ENROUTE
Make the time

En Route Books and Media, LLC
5705 Rhodes Avenue
St. Louis, MO 63109

ISBN: 979-8-88870-419-6
Library of Congress Control Number: Online https://catalog.loc.gov

To a Younger Brother

Eric Gilhooly, LC

En Route Books and Media, LLC
Saint Louis, MO

Cover design by Timothy D. Boatright
Vistra Communications
Tampa, Florida

Thy Kingdom Come!

Dedicated to all the companions I've had during my years of preparation for the priesthood. Once a brother, always a brother!

Table of Contents

FOREWORD

May I begin with a note of gratitude to Eric Gilhooly, LC who recently was ordained a transitional deacon as a member of the Legion of Christ. He has written *To a Younger Brother* in 2018 as a series of inspiring reflections for seminarians who are studying for the priesthood. It is dedicated to all the companions he has had during his own years of preparation for the priesthood. He writes, "Once a brother, always a brother!"

I am delighted that Eric has invited me to write this foreword for such a mission he has undertaken at this time to offer his personal support and guidance to those men who are in our seminaries throughout the world. He himself has a deep personal relationship with Jesus Christ as His missionary disciple within the Legion of Christ.

When I was in Rome as a priest member working in the Congregation for the Clergy in the year 2000, I was ordained a bishop by now Pope Saint John Paul II. He called all of us to missionary discipleship with the words "Be Not Afraid!" Since my call to the episcopate, I have served until 2008 in the Diocese of Cheyenne, Wyoming, when I accepted the call to the Diocese of Green Bay, Wisconsin, where I am in my tenth year as the diocesan bishop. Every bishop, in union with all priests and those studying to become priests, works closely with appointed vocation directors. Without a doubt, the need for good priests is always a top priority throughout the world.

In this urgent context, *To a Younger Brother* is invaluable in assisting each seminarian in his journey to the priesthood. Eric Gilhooly, LC writes his personal reflections on his continuing path to the priesthood with genuine loving compassion. As a seminarian of many years with varied experiences in Ireland, Rome, and the United States, Eric speaks candidly about his relationship with Christ through his years thus far in human and spiritual growth. He extends these reflections to all of his brother seminarians all over the world.

Each of the sixteen short chapters in the book reveals Eric's deep and solid commitment to a personal relationship with Christ through prayer as the foundation for everything the Holy Spirit, as master artist of souls, offers to his fellow seminarians. It is evident throughout his book of personal reflections that, in the spirit of Pope Francis, Eric envisions the Church today as a call to be missionary disciples for Christ. Clearly, the truth lived out in love is so strong that the reader is drawn in as well.

After reading a book of meditations I wrote for priests in 2009, entitled *Be Thou My Vision*, Eric expressed to me how it has influenced his ongoing seminary formation as a living encounter with God as the hallmark of priestly existence. In his own words, he affirms that you can reach spiritual maturity only once you have learned to let the Holy Spirit guide your life. Even more directly, he sees adventure, beauty, and freedom in God as life in Christ. The author's deep regard for his fellow seminarians in the freely chosen celibate life of the priesthood is admirable. Many literary references and diverse recommended readings in the chapters are offered to seminarians as living examples to illustrate concretely what can inspire seminarians today.

It is within the deep intimacy of the Holy Eucharist that the author of *To a Younger Brother* enters into his spirituality which is extended to regular Adoration of Jesus in the Blessed Sacrament. In a "down-to-earth" way of speaking to seminarians, he says that " . . . the Eucharist is like the microwave for sanctity. Simply being in Jesus's presence transforms me little by little."

To a Younger Brother is both a helpful and inspiring guide, especially today, for all seminarians who are desperately searching for peace, love, and joy that comes from Jesus Christ who loves us now and forever. I invite and encourage seminarians and other interested readers to let *To a Younger Brother* open up the mystery of God to live missionary discipleship in service to all of God's people.

Most Reverend David L. Ricken, DD, JCL
Bishop of Green Bay, Wisconsin
July 2018

Introduction

I am the oldest of seven kids . . . and the only boy. I remember growing up longing for a brother; and every time my mom was pregnant, I was sure that it was my little brother finally on his way. Well, God sent me quite a few sisters but so far, no brother. As time passed, I felt budding within me the desire to give my life to God as his priest. Years later, as a seminarian, I was given the opportunity to accompany several younger seminarians as an academic tutor and discovered that God had given me the gift of being an older brother for them. Finally!

Once, I read this book by a priest who called himself a professional seminarian: he had been one for ten years. So, I said to myself, "Eric, if he can call himself a professional seminarian after ten years, well, after four years in a minor seminary and what will be fifteen in major seminary, you have every right to call yourself a professional seminarian."

I had two years of novitiate in Ireland, two years of humanities studies in the US, four years of philosophy in Rome, four years of apostolic internship back in the US, and am studying three years of theology in Rome—a bit longer than most of my companions! Maybe these years have not always been "professional," but I like to think I have gotten something out of them!

So, I started to reflect on what I have lived and the many opportunities I have had to share experiences with my fellow seminarians . . . and here you have this book. There are books by priests directed to seminarians and books by bishops or priests or lay people directed to priests, but never seminarian-to-seminarian, brother-to-brother.

This book is written by a seminarian for seminarians on a variety of topics: some I've spent years reflecting on and discussing; others, I felt I had to include no matter what. And, of course, there are many more not included here.

At times, the experiences I describe in these pages are what I've lived or that are common to a lot of seminarians, but not necessarily a one-size-fits-all. The most important thing is getting from what may be more subjective in my experiences and reflections to Christ Himself, the foundation and guarantee of our priesthood. You might not want to read this book from beginning to end but skip directly to what helps you. Then, then take time to pray and reflect. At the end of each chapter, I have included a selection of books I have read myself and recommended to others; they will help you go a lot deeper than I could ever bring you in these pages.

And for the record, I will remorselessly spoil the endings of different novels and movies that help me get across what I am trying to say. No complaining. You have been fairly warned.

I finished this book in May 2018, a few weeks before being ordained a deacon. Everything here has been written as a seminarian—as a brother. Andrew brought his brother Peter to Jesus through sharing his experience and conviction:

"Andrew, the brother of Simon Peter, was one of the two who heard John and followed Jesus. He first found his own brother Simon and told him, 'We have found the Messiah' (which is translated Anointed). Then he brought him to Jesus" (John 1:40-42). Peter followed Jesus and became the rock on which Jesus built His Church.

So, my prayer for you is that you come to more fully understand and grow in this calling you have been given. May you fall more deeply in love with your vocation and with Our Lord. You have given up everything to follow Jesus; may He Himself be your prize in this life and the next!

Your brother in Christ,

Eric Gilhooly, LC
December 8, 2021

Chapter 1
What It Takes

3 September 1971. Sergei Kourdakov had been in the icy waves for at least three hours. Risking everything to escape, he had jumped from his Soviet ship in the middle of a stormy night to swim for the Canadian shore some three and a half miles away.

Now, just as his strength was giving out, he saw, to his horror, that he had swum in a circle and was again before the very ship he had abandoned. He refused to consider allowing himself to be taken back by the Russians aboard. Feebly striking out once more, he realized he had no idea in which direction the shore lay. He was going to drown.[1]

Taking Stock

And me? Do I have what it takes? Will I be able to make it to that distant coastline? Every young person making a life choice—beginning a career or getting married—asks himself this question. As a tendential control freak, I ask it to myself before I decide to do almost anything. And in order to answer it, I need to look at the task: What will it require? What are the steps I will have to follow to get it done? How much will it cost in time, effort, and money? Against those requirements, I then compare myself: Am I strong enough, smart enough? Am I willing and able to pay the price?

Jesus Himself counseled prudence: "what king marching into battle would not first sit down and decide whether with ten thousand troops he can successfully oppose another king advancing upon him with twenty thousand troops?" (Lk 14:31)

When it comes to a priestly vocation, these are essential questions in any discernment process. We need a clear idea of the radicalness Christ asks of us and a willingness to give Him everything and follow Him anywhere. We must know, at least in theory if not experientially, what it means to accept our vocation and embrace the Cross of Christ. Of course, following Christ always means more than we had expected; the future will surprise us, and like Sergei, we may find ourselves sinking in icy-cold water . . . And then, we ask ourselves if we have what it takes to live this vocation. Especially at the beginning of following Christ, we can fall into the temptation of relying too much on our own strength.

Our relationship with God and others could fall into a type of business category: God asks me to do A, B, and C; I do A, B, and C, so I am a good person, a holy person. I fulfill my contract with God. This is practical Pelagianism: a do-it-yourself kind of salvation, living by a contract we imagine that we have with God and others. My hope lies in my own effort and work. This leads me to calculate everything in my relationship with God: I have given Him this much; therefore, He owes me a deep prayer life, virtue, etc., and He can ask of me only so much.

As for my companions or those I work with, they obviously are not as generous and holy as I am because they do not do all the things I do for God—they are not "faithful." So I either judge them harshly or feel toward them a condescending pity. The result? My heart, little by little, becomes hardened toward others. "Whoever does not love a brother whom he has seen cannot love God whom he has not seen" (1 Jn 4:20).

Despair or Hope

And then . . . it happens. God allows failure in my life: my projects collapse, or I fall into sin. I realize, to my horror (and through God's grace), that I am weak and that I cannot follow Him with perfection. I cannot reach the virtue to which I am called. I cannot live out my priestly vocation in fidelity. The illusions I have created of myself and of the world around me shatter, and the whole situation can throw me into shock or panic. What will I do now? What can be done? There seems to be no way out.

My first reaction might be to blame it all on God: Is He really all powerful? Does He even exist? And while I might intellectually accept His objective power and existence, it becomes awfully hard to believe in His goodness, that He actually loves me. I mean, if He really loved me, He never would have let me fall. I have done so much for Him—if He were a good God, He would keep His end of the bargain and not abandon me when I most need Him.

It's a make-or-break moment that either leads to despair or to hope. If I learn to accept myself—and that includes my weakness, my failure, and my need for help—I can learn to be at peace with who I am in all my fragility. Then, the only solution is God. He becomes my only hope above and beyond any talents I have or any work I do. I ask for and receive His mercy, and that changes everything.

Right after the verse about having enough men to defeat a rival king, Jesus continues: "In the same way, everyone of you who does not renounce all his possessions cannot be my disciple" (Lk 14:33). So, part of our calculation implies leaving behind everything . . . including our "ten thousand troops"! Once we leave it all, we can add Christ's omnipotence to our nothingness, and all things become possible. You almost feel sorry for that other king with just twenty thousand.

Getting back to Sergei's story as he tells it in *Forgive Me, Natasha*, at that moment of accepting his death, he turned to God and made his first prayer ever. At once, new strength entered him; and he knew in what direction he had to swim. After over five hours total in the freezing ocean, he made it to shore. Sergei, who for many years had persecuted Christians in Russia, later asked for Baptism.[2]

What are the consequences of this experience of powerlessness and mercy in my own life? First of all, I can start a true relationship with God based on who He is and who I am—not what I do or can give Him. This relationship is not founded on a contract but on His undeserved love that I have experienced in my own life and my own deep, deep gratitude for his mercy.

I grow out of the artificial business relationship into a relationship of family: God is my Father, and I am His child. I rely on Him for everything; and, like a child, I do everything I can to make Him happy. I work, pray, and preach; but it is all rooted in an unbreakable trust in Him. And from that trust flow a profound joy and peace.

"Let those who fear the Lord say, his mercy endures forever. In danger I called on the Lord; the Lord answered me and set me free" (Ps 118:4-5).

This experience of having been forgiven, of not having what it takes, forms in us a priestly heart: a heart that sees and understands that others are weak, that does not judge or condemn but eagerly invites all men and women to enter into God's freeing mercy. So, through our weakness and our failings, God can give us what we need to reach out to others and become apostles of mercy: *Come and live what I've lived! Jesus is real! He's alive, and He loves you!*

Recommended Reading

Abandonment to Divine Providence by Jean-Pierre de Caussade. This author invites us to put everything in God's hands—a lesson of trust.

The Lord of the Rings by J. R. R. Tolkien. I put this book here as a tale of success through failure. Frodo "fails" in his mission of destroying the Ring, yet he does what he can, and his true success is found in his learning mercy, especially toward Gollum.

Spe Salvi (*Saved in Hope*) by Benedict XVI. This is my favorite encyclical by Pope Emeritus Benedict, helping us to look beyond this world toward God so we can overcome cynicism and discouragement through supernatural hope.

NOTES

1. Sergei Kourdakov, *Forgive Me, Natasha* (New York: Harper Collins, 1975).
2. Ibid.

CHAPTER 2
MY WOUNDS, HIS STRENGTH

I was halfway through my second year of philosophy when my congregation, the Legion of Christ, told us that our founder had been an abuser. Doubt and sorrow tore through all our hearts. We had thought of him as a saint, as a model to imitate, and now . . .

Broken . . .

Everyone bears a wounded heart; and as a future priest, you are called to help Jesus bring healing into so many people's lives: through Confession, a word of advice, or simply listening. But wait! If everyone has wounds, that means you do, too—you are not perfect. Sooner or later, you will have to come face to face with yourself in all your weakness. You may not like what you see.

I have met and lived alongside seminarians whose parents have divorced, who have been betrayed by those they trusted or been rejected by those they looked up to. Others of us have to struggle every day just to get out of bed and make it to the chapel for morning prayer—and fail as often as not. Some try with everything they have to do well in studies and, well, you cannot give much more than everything, can you?

And all of us have to deal with sin in our lives: the past that haunts us, the overwhelming temptations of the present, or simply those petty vices that will not go away however many times we try and weed them out.

If you let your wounds define you, you become a permanent victim—you remain paralyzed. It's like breaking your arm and then ignoring it because it hurts too much to touch. You leave it to heal as it is or, perhaps, set it badly; and at best, you can hope to get by, but it will never be like it once was. A broken limb left to itself will affect the rest of your life. If you pretend your wounds do not exist, they will lead you anywhere from frustration to despair. Then, you might even try to solve things by lashing out, making others victims to forget the pain.

Yet Blessed

But what happens when I face my wounds (not by myself, but together with Jesus!)? Sure, we know that God loves us and He forgives us; but that belief leads us to the foot of the Cross. There, we encounter the Crucified Lord who says to us, "Come, all who pass by the way, pay attention and see: Is there any pain like my pain . . . ?" (Lam 1:12). Yet Jesus has chosen His Cross freely, for my sake, to win me my forgiveness.

Remember the scene in Mel Gibson's *The Passion of the Christ* when Jesus has just been crucified? One of the priests mocks Him: " . . . save yourself, if you are the son of God, come down from the cross!" (Mt 27:40) And with a leer of triumph before the crowd, he turns his back on Jesus. Jesus hears. He lifts His eyes upwards and first in a whisper, then louder, says "Father, forgive them, they know not what they do" (Lk 23:34). The priest stops dead in his tracks. "Listen!" cries the Good Thief, "He's praying for you!" But instead of turning back to Jesus, the priest keeps walking away from Him.

I don't have to be like that Pharisee! I don't have to walk away from Jesus when He offers His mercy but can turn back and let the Cross change my life. I am forgiven, and I am loved.

On the Cross, Christ shouts out that not only has He taken all my sin on Himself but also all my wounds. There on Calvary, I can unite my wounds to His so His strength and grace can fill me and give me courage to go on. And often, it is at Calvary where God pours out the healing He so longs to give me. "Within your wounds, shelter me!"[1]

After hearing the news about our founder, I remember going to a small side chapel by myself—crying, begging God to tell me why, while at the same time, knowing that I would never be able to understand. During that visit, I received a grace that not only helped me get through the crisis of those years but sustains me still. I did not know if our congregation would be dissolved or what might happen. But that visit brought home one certainty as all my other certainties crumbled: Christ is faithful. And whatever happens, He will be there with me and will give me the grace to keep on following Him. To Jesus and Jesus alone have I given my life. I think this moment of woundedness helped me center my life more on Christ and little by little, rely on His strength alone.

Christ will not explain away our wounds but bear them with us, sanctifying them and turning them into channels of grace for ourselves and for others. "I have prayed that your own faith may not fail; and once you have turned back, you must strengthen your brothers" (Lk 22:32). The Gospels of Luke and John tell us that when Jesus appeared to His Apostles after the Resurrection, His wounds were still there, part of His glorified body. They prove to us that He really suffered and that His wounds have eternal value—"By his wounds we were healed" (Isaiah 53:5). Having united our wounds to Christ's gives us the strength to be a channel of grace for others through those very wounds.

For a priest, this experience of our wounds united to Christ is invaluable! You have been called to dispense God's mercy to His children, especially through Confession: the ultimate experience of mercy. As another Christ, you can only convincingly offer a mercy you have experienced—use the "product" you are trying to sell. Getting on your knees each week or two helps you remember who you are, leading to humility and compassion for others; it reminds you that your strength is in Christ alone. Confession is a sacrament of conversion—your pastoral work must be sacramental or it will not have lasting value.

The Cross wipes away sin and overcomes weakness. This needing Jesus and His mercy leads us to be humble, to accept and even laugh at ourselves. It gives us a heart for others that understands weakness and knows how to transmit spiritual strength. We must teach our souls to receive grace through their crosses!

You may have read the book *Left to Tell* by Immaculée Ilibagiza. In it, she describes the horrible ordeal of the Rwandan genocide and how she grew in her relationship with God. Several years after the holocaust, she returned to her hometown and confronted Felician, the imprisoned leader of the gang who had killed her family.

At their meeting, the prison guard screamed derisively at Felician, who hunched over in shame, unable to meet Immaculée's eyes. Immaculée reached out and touched him, and as she looked into his tear-stained face, whispered, "I forgive you."[2]

God has taken Immaculée and her terrible sufferings—beyond anything you and I are ever likely to experience—and is using her as a means to spread His message of forgiveness. God saved her, she says, so that she could share her story and help as many as possible to experience the healing of forgiveness.[3]

We must all "rewrite" our personal stories, not in the sense of changing the past but in learning to see our lives through God's eyes and finding His grace that has led us. How can you do this? There are many possible ways, but I would like to mention just one: Ignatian Spiritual Exercises. They come in many formats, but if you are used to day retreats, I would strongly suggest you do at least the week-long version. This incredibly grace-filled experience helps put your personal story within the history of salvation and invites you to enter into the mystery of Christ. You place your past in its wider context of grace and mercy and learn to trace God's finger along your life's path, thus discovering its true meaning (this is the biblical memory that Pope Francis mentions so often). You are helped to fall deeper in love with Jesus and imitate Him more closely—direction for the present and hope for the future. So the exercises are meant quite literally to be a life-defining experience.

You have wounds. Those wounds will prove too great to bear unless you unite them to Christ and through the Cross, await resurrection.

> But he said to me, "My grace is sufficient for you, for power is made perfect in weakness." I will rather boast most gladly of my weaknesses, in order that the power of Christ may dwell with me. Therefore, I am content with weaknesses, insults, hardships, persecutions, and constraints, for the sake of Christ; for when I am weak, then I am strong. (2 Cor 12:9-10)

Recommended Reading

Be Healed: A Guide to Encountering the Powerful Love of Jesus in Your Life by Bob Schuchts. God wants His children to be completely healed, and often we need to help people overcome their deepest wounds so God can enter into their lives.

The Return of the Prodigal Son: A Story of Homecoming by Henri J. M. Nouwen. This is a classic book on conversion based on Rembrandt's painting.

The Sadness of Christ by Thomas More. This book was written shortly before his martyrdom to find strength in weakness.

Stronger than Hate: Struggling to Forgive by Tim Guénard. This book is a true story of terrible suffering and the strength to forgive found in Christ.

NOTES

1. See the "Anima Christi."
2. Immaculée Ilibagiza, *Left to Tell* (Carlsbad, CA: Hay House, 2010), 203-204.
3. Ibid., 208-209.

CHAPTER 3
A LOVER OF THE CROSS

I don't know about you, but when people speak about their suffering, my tendency is to answer, to give them something from my tremendous store of spiritual "wisdom" and "experience" because *talking* about hardship is easy. Advising others on how to keep the faith and overcome their trials . . . is easy.

Theory and Reality

When we first fell in love with Christ and decided to follow Him, I am sure we all did it with high ideals, often imagining the great things we would do for Him. This is a good thing. Like the saints, we expect we will suffer tremendously, stay strong in the faith in spite of all obstacles, and, perhaps, even be martyred.

Our dreams are dramatic, heroic, and, naturally, very well planned out. Of course, we will accept the trials, but they will come at such-and-such a moment, when I expect them, will last so much time, will happen in such a manner. This suffering we imagine and theoretically accept has very little cross in it, with so many conditions and terms that we would barely feel it if God were to follow our proposals.

We can react in so many ways to pain but with indifference is not one of them. Tragedy is tragedy precisely because no one can plan for it; no one can understand it or fit it into a neat and rational category. That is just what happened with Our Lord. Before the Cross, all His disciples flee, and Peter explicitly denies Jesus—just the night before he had sworn that he was ready to die with Him! The two on the road to Emmaus feel betrayed since their plans had not been fulfilled: before the Cross, *we had hoped . . .* [1]

Why is it that God makes Himself present only after we have been cast into the fiery furnace? Why only after the bread has been broken? The cross cannot be planned out, and it hits us where we are weakest. It hurts, and no rationalization or spiritual discourse can change that or make stoics out of us. But who wants to be a stoic?

Joseph Ratzinger writes that stoics try to avoid suffering by leaving it behind as something alien and dominating it through self-control. He continues: "Christ does not die in the noble detachment of the philosopher. He dies in tears. On his lips was the bitter taste of abandonment and isolation in all its horror."[2]

Jesus on Calvary was not how we would like to imagine ourselves at our deaths—heroic, full of the expansive faith and unquenchable joy that many of the martyrs were graced with. Not Jesus. Why would I want anything else for myself?

When sorrow brings me to my knees, I realize just how weak I am. I can either turn on God or turn toward Him. I can accuse Him of not loving me and say that he probably does not even exist; or I can run into His arms like a little child. Only faith can help me overcome moments of suffering without growing bitter—knowing that there is no explanation I could possibly understand right now but trusting in God.

No matter what God allows, He will never let me fall out of His hands. "I was appointed preacher and apostle and teacher. On this account I am suffering these things; but I am not ashamed, for I know him in whom I have believed and am confident that he is able to guard what has been entrusted to me until that day." (2 Tm 1:11-12). He has loved and protected me in the past—I have experienced it—I know he will not abandon me now. Even in suffering and often because of it, we can come out stronger in our faith in God. And united with Jesus, our suffering becomes cross: an instrument of redemption.

I remember several years ago, I was on a door-to-door mission in Connecticut to invite people to come back to Church. Another seminarian and I stopped in front of a light blue house with a two-door garage and a floor with the living quarters on top. A couple, both about sixty years old, met us on the driveway, and we began to chat. I do not remember their exact situation. A loved one had died or they had lost contact with their children . . . whatever it was, they had suffered a lot.

I was very confused inside and had no idea what to say to them. Who was I to try to give them a word of consolation? I ended up promising to pray for them. Their faces lit up at once, and their eyes filled with joy as, between huge smiles, they thanked me again and again. These people taught me so much about what lived faith means. Prayers would not take away the suffering, but they would make it bearable.

One thing you can do to prepare for those moments of suffering is meditate on Christ Crucified: ask Him why He is suffering and what secrets are in His heart as He hangs on the Cross. Hear Him whisper that His suffering is for your sake and is God's greatest cry of love . . . Then the Cross becomes the most beautiful moment in history. What could be more beautiful than entering right into the depth of God's desperately crazy love?

"Do not fear, for I have redeemed you; I have called you by name: you are mine. When you pass through waters, I will be with you; through rivers, you shall not be swept away. When you walk through fire, you shall not be burned, nor will flames consume you" (Is 43:1-2).

Fruits

So what about the afterwards? What spiritual benefits or Resurrection graces does God give His future priest through the Cross? The Cross helps us to mature spiritually. We become more identified with Jesus and grow in our faith. The Cross teaches us the essential in life: only God. Everything else passes. In this way, our love is purified.

We see this realization of what really matters happen in the 2012 movie *The Impossible*, a true-life story of Maria, Henry, and their children during the 2004 tsunami. Before disaster floods their vacation, the dad, Henry, is worried about locking his home, about his economic situation, and his job. They have a very materialistic Christmas, and the elder son, Lucas, seems to have a bit of an attitude. After they are separated, Maria and Lucas are rescued together with another child they find, and Lucas starts to try and help reunite family members separated by the disaster.

Henry must bring his two younger sons to safety and search for the other half of his family. Throughout the film, there is no direct reference to God, yet there are frequent shots that begin viewing the wreckage and turmoil around and slowly move up toward the peaceful sky. This "looking up" gets the family through the crisis.

The final scene shows the family together on the plane home. Whereas before there had been slight divisions and pettiness, now they have been firmly united. "How are you?" Maria asks Lucas as she grabs his hand from the stretcher where she lies strapped down for the trip. Tears fill both their eyes. "Here with you," he replies.[3]

Having suffered opens your heart to others who suffer: to the poor, the sick, the abandoned—to those who think life is not worth it or have lost faith in a loving God. Everyone has their share of grief; and as a priest, called to identify yourself with Jesus Priest and Victim, you will often have to weep and take your shoes off before the holy ground of sorrow.

The Cross accepted in faith, for the sake of Christ, with and in Him, allows you to live the hardest moments in great peace, transforming those moments into the most beautiful and fruitful of your life.

A few years ago, I was helping a younger seminarian in academic tutoring, and we struck up a friendship. Every once in a while, we would talk about the vocation. He was not sure God was calling him to the priesthood and felt frustrated because of the tension between the seminary rules and how he wanted to live. On his twenty-first birthday, we spoke and he was really in the dumps—what was he doing with his life? Was it all a waste?

That night, before going to bed, I made a visit to Mary for him; and I asked her for the grace to take a bit of the suffering off the other guy's shoulders and give it to me. And in a sense, she did: extra sacrifices and difficulties here and there. My life did not become unbearable by any stretch, but it did become more of a gift. Months later, the other seminarian discerned God was calling him to lay life. When we spoke about it, the topic of his birthday came up; and he told me that that very night God had given him a lot of peace and the conviction that wherever God led him, the key to his life was living in love.

Jesus calls you, a future priest, to be Simon: to help others bear their crosses as they walk their Calvary. The Cross is your right! And only God knows how many souls will be touched and uplifted thanks to the crosses God gives you to bear. Only God knows how much each of us has been helped by others' prayer and sacrifice. Your cross, like Our Lord's, is for the sake of those entrusted to you: your life laid down as victim with and in Jesus.

"Unless a grain of wheat falls to the ground and dies, it remains just a grain of wheat; but if it dies, it produces much fruit. Whoever loves his life loses it, and whoever hates his life in this world will preserve it for eternal life. Whoever serves me must follow me, and where I am, there also will my servant be" (Jn 12:24-26).

Recommended Reading

A Severe Mercy by Sheldon Vanauken. This is a true story of love, conversion, and suffering; coming to grips with the meaning of the Cross.

Walking with God through Pain and Suffering by Timothy Keller. This book discusses entering into the experience of suffering and points out attitudes that help us deepen in our understanding of it.

Till We Have Faces: A Myth Retold by C. S. Lewis. This novel deals with the question of evil and how God could allow it; human loves and how they need to be purified.

A Grief Observed by C. S. Lewis. This comes from his diary, written after the death of his wife as he tries to come to grips with his terrible loss.

NOTES

1. See Luke 24:21.
2. Joseph Ratzinger, *Eschatology: Death and Eternal Life* (Washington, DC: The Catholic University of America Press, 1988), 102.
3. *The Impossible.* Directed by J. A. Bayona. Burbank, CA: Warner Brothers, 2012.

CHAPTER 4
THE SECRET WITHIN THE MIRACLE: CELIBACY FOR THE KINGDOM OF GOD

In his book *Till We Have Faces*, C. S. Lewis tells the tale of a beautiful princess, Psyche, who has been chosen by lot to be sacrificed to the gods in order to end a drought in the kingdom of Glome. In their terminology, she will be "wedded" to the god. And to her sister Orual's anger and confusion, Psyche is actually happy about it! How could she rejoice in her family's being torn apart and in her own death? Told from the sister's point of view:

> "Oh, Psyche," I said, almost in a shriek, "what can these things be except the cowardly murder they seem?" . . . "I see," said Psyche in a low voice. "You think it devours the offering. I mostly think so myself. Anyway, it means death. Orual, you didn't think I was such a child as not to know that? How can I be a ransom for all Glome unless I die? And if I am to go to the god, of course it must be through death. That way, even what is strangest in the holy sayings might be true. To be eaten and to be married to the god might not be so different."[1]

Is our own call to celibacy any less dramatic? Does it seem any less absurd to those who look at our vocation without eyes of faith?

In Matthew 19:12, Jesus tells us about those who "have renounced marriage for the sake of the kingdom of heaven." Jesus Himself lived this lifestyle as did Saint Paul. And in our Roman Catholic rite, those who follow Christ as His priests are also asked to live in this way, for the sake of the Kingdom of Heaven.

Any priest and seminarian who is honest will admit that living celibately is difficult. So what are we dealing with when we talk about celibacy as vocation and charism—much more than a mere discipline?

A Big Heart

If you have been called to the priesthood, it is because God has given you a very big heart, a heart big enough for all the people God is planning to put on your path. Now, having a big heart opens us to great and deep desires. We want to give ourselves for others, to die in order to give life. When we look at Jesus, nothing seems too much to sacrifice in order to love Him and to bring Him to as many souls as possible.

A big heart also means an urgent and consuming need for intimacy. A series of day-to-day work relationships or acquaintances will never be enough to fill that gaping hole. Intimacy means to know another's secrets, their desires and dreams and gifts; it means to be known completely as I am, to accept and be accepted without condition. Intimacy means union. Anything else is a pale substitute.

So, my big heart and my need for intimacy will pull me toward other people. I will feel attracted to women, and that will sometimes cause me to struggle with my call to celibacy. Some might give in to porn or masturbation. It can happen—just because you start to follow Jesus does not mean you stop being a man or stop having temptations! "My child, when you come to serve the Lord, prepare yourself for trials" (Sir 2:1).

Our hearts are hard to control, and they try to attach themselves to any and everything. We rein them in and try to direct them where we want to go; and then the next minute, they are bucking like a wild stallion, and all we can do is try and hang on. That we feel these temptations and inclinations is not itself bad; that we accept and act on them is.

A big heart recognizes the beauty of marriage and of building a family. A man was made to be with a woman: "It is not good for the man to be alone" (Gn 2:18). Marriage—finding the right person with whom I can share everything and who needs me to protect, defend, and cherish her—is an incredible miracle, a living sign of God's love for humanity. God blesses it and uses one spouse to sustain the other on their journey toward Him.

And then, children! True love cannot be contained, or else it grows stagnant. Couples express this especially through their children who are a gift to the world, and they themselves become a gift for their children and are made whole through this self-giving. I could go on and on about how wonderful marriage is and what an awesome calling God has given the great majority of humanity. Pray about it, and stand in awe before the mystery.

We were made for love, given a big heart and the need for intimacy. Yet if we are not doing what God created man and woman for, will that not lead to frustration? We have so much to offer the world; and yet at times, do we not feel stunted?

Living a celibate life, for some, can imply living *in spite of* our huge heart and its passions that try to drag us in and out like the tide. One reaction to our hearts is to try and repress them, to cut them off from all desire so we can live a peaceful, untroubled life. Scared of losing control, we establish a totalitarian regime in our lives, intent on conquering the slightest dissent. Of course, no dictatorship that oppresses its subjects can last long. In the end, the contained pressure becomes too much, and rebellions and protests explode as a reaction to the suppression.

When I try to cut off my desires, to cut out my heart, I am cutting away at myself and at what God created me to be. The priests of Israel had to be complete, without any blemish (see Lv 21:17-23). God does not want half-men serving Him. He calls us to be whole.

Wholly Celibate

When we ignore our attraction to women or focus on the long list of "don'ts" that our vocation implies, it gets very depressing very quickly. So how can we live our calling to celibacy without destroying our hearts?

Priests are not the only people who have to say no to things that they are pulled toward by their passions. A married man has to say no to every woman he sees passing by him on the street or on the internet. But his seemingly endless list of little nos finds its proper meaning and context only within one overwhelming *yes*. "For where your treasure is, there also will your heart be" (Mt 6:21). He is in love with his wife, and that changes everything. If he is really committed to and crazy about his wife, then all the other little nos are simply a necessary consequence, not a paralyzing obsession.

A guy in love does not care if he "wastes" money on flowers or if he misses his favorite television show so he can take his wife out to dinner. He risks any and everything for her because she has become his life. Sure, there will be times that he will need to struggle more, to fight in order to be faithful to his yes, but that fight becomes something positive, a strengthening of his heart in its decision to love and be completely intimate with one woman alone who is the love of his life. He does not always feel it; but in that moment, he proves his love.

A priest has to love God like crazy. At times, he will not seem to experience that love, but he still needs to ask for the grace of a madly overwhelming love for Jesus that leaves no room for any other love. If our hearts are not completely centered on Christ, we easily start to attach ourselves to little things, little concessions here and there that can end up destroying us.

"You shall love the Lord your God with all your heart, with all your soul, with all your mind, and with all your strength" (Mk 12:30). Jesus is pretty clear: all or nothing. And it makes sense. What man could tell his wife, "I will love you completely Monday through Friday, but Saturday nights are for me and someone else." It will not work!

Bishop David Ricken writes, "The celibate deprives himself of the crowning act of his manhood. If that vacuum is not filled with something that carries joy at its very roots, the deprivation and emptiness will almost be too much to bear."[2]

Jesus has to be a real person for me—an idea of God will not be anywhere near enough to fill my heart. We can have intimacy only with another person. And how can we become intimate with Jesus, to get to share His innermost secrets and desires? We learn in our studies that charity is a theological virtue—love for God is something we cannot get on our own but receive as a grace. God wants to give me this grace, so He has decided to get very close to us.

I love the song "A Sky Full of Stars" by Coldplay—go ahead; look it up, and listen to it.

Most people who hear this song would think of a man singing to the woman he loves. His love is beautiful because she is so beautiful; she could be compared to the endless beauty of the skies.

Now, try this: go back over the song's words and read them (or sing them) as a prayer directed to God. God made the sky! He made the stars! All creation whispers to us the secret of who made it—someone much greater! A heavenly view: to see God in everything and to seek God in everything. The song takes on a much deeper and truer meaning when we say, "God, *you* are a sky full of stars. I want to die in *your* arms." In the same way, dedicating our hearts to God alone completes and deepens who we are.

You can tell where someone's heart is by what he does when he has extra time. Some things in life we simply have to do, and there is no getting around them. But when I can choose, what do I do? That says a lot about my heart.

Someone who is in love with Jesus (or wants to fall in love with Him) spends a lot of time with Him, especially in the Eucharist. Jesus Himself enters into me at each Mass, waits silently for me in the tabernacle, longs to see me, to embrace me. We also have God's Word and many other times for prayer. We yearn to speak with Him in the intimacy of our hearts throughout the day. "My soul thirsts for God, the living God. When can I enter and see the face of God?" (Ps 42:3)

This personal, real, and passionate love for Christ gives me joy and inner freedom as I live my celibacy. Celibacy helps me be faithful to him as my only love in life—it is a supernatural calling. The stoics tried to live celibacy (more or less successfully) through repression, but a priest's heart must be the Heart of Jesus for others—it has to be alive!

When our hearts are completely focused on the One we love, then we learn to mold our hearts according to His and to love what He loves as He loves it. So, we say no to other possibilities of exclusive relationships, and this opens our hearts in order to be able to love everyone as Jesus loves them, completely and unselfishly. We can unite ourselves with Christ in His love for the Church, and this is truly a spousal love: "Husbands, love your wives, even as Christ loved the church and handed himself over for her" (Eph 5:25).

Through celibacy, God calls me to find personal fulfillment through love and to become a gift for others.

Recommended Reading

Desire: The Journey We Must Take to Find the Life God Offers by John Eldredge (especially chapters 8-10). This book helps you fall in love with Jesus (again) and renew your longing for heaven.

Be Thou My Vision by David Ricken (especially chapter 3). This is the best book I have read on the priesthood, chapter 3 being the best thing I have read on celibacy.

And You Are Christ's: The Charism of Virginity and the Celibate Life by Thomas Dubay, S.M. Written specifically for female religious, this book looks at the beauty of virginity from the perspective of the Gospels and Carmelite spirituality.

Sacerdotalis Caelibatus (On the Celibacy of the Priest) by Saint Paul VI. This is a well-articulated and inspiring treatment of the theme.

NOTES

1. C. S. Lewis, *Till We Have Faces* (Orlando: Harcourt Brace & Company, 1984), 71-72.
2. David L. Ricken, *Be Thou My Vision* (Omaha: IPF Publications, 2009), 44.

Chapter 5
Not Alone:
Companions for the Journey

The Lord of the Rings tells of the One Ring, shaped to dominate all and bend everything to the evil will of the dark lord Sauron. Unless it is destroyed, cast into the fire in which it was made, all Middle Earth must fall.

When Frodo, the story's protagonist, offers to bear the Ring alone into Sauron's domain in order to destroy it, he is not sent by himself but given companions. They freely offer to join him on his quest, though no one else can take his place, and not all will survive the journey. The mission, Frodo is told, belongs to him alone. He alone has the duty to bear the Ring to Mount Doom and cast it into the flame. He alone must protect it at all cost from Sauron and the dark lord's servants. Others have chosen to accompany Frodo on his quest: a wizard, several hobbits, men, a dwarf, and an elf. None will vow to complete the quest, says Elrond, for none of them knows the strength of his heart and what tests they may meet on the journey. They must accompany Frodo yet are free to turn back or turn aside to other paths.

You have an impossible quest, a vocation that you cannot fulfill alone—the priesthood is beyond you. Of course, you will rely on God, but God has willed that you rely on others.

Our culture today tells us that men need to be tough. Any show of emotion or weakness means that you are simply not up to the job, that you do not have what it takes and are not worth the respect of your peers. We are taught to be very individualistic, and not only in a selfish look-out-for-number-one kind of way: rely on no one but yourself because if you let down your guard or depend on anyone else, you will be betrayed. You will fail.

I have already shared with you some reflections on how we need to trust in God. Now I would like to focus on our relationships with others. It would be so much easier if my holiness were just something between Jesus and me: I could work hard, grow, and become more worthy of Him. Yes, I would deal with others, but Jesus would completely fill my heart, so there would be no need for close friends, right? I could deal directly with God.

Well, I have news for you: you are human. And "human" means entering into countless relationships with others. Part of God's plan and how He wants to work in your life requires that you have some very close friendships that help you along the journey.

When Jesus came to earth, He did not visit each person and say, "Hey! I'm God, and I'm going to die and rise again to show you how much I love you. Change your life; follow Me, and I will take you to heaven to be perfectly happy." Jesus could have done that; but instead, He founded His Church, His community made up of men and women meant to help each other know Him better. And He sent them out: "Go, therefore, and make disciples of all nations, baptizing them in the name of the Father, and of the Son, and of the Holy Spirit, teaching them to observe all that I have commanded you" (Mt 28:19-20). We know about Jesus and can enter into relationship with Him because others have helped us to do so. That is how it will always be while this world lasts.

In our specific case—the seminary—we have the grace of belonging to a community of other seminarians, a miniature local Church. We fight and form ourselves alongside men who share our ideals and dreams, who work toward the same goals and carry many of the same crosses. We are brothers in arms and brothers in Christ. As in any family or community, we will have fights and disagreements. There is no ideal community. But the brothers you have are those you have been given by God and those who will help you during these years of intense preparation for what will be your life's work: your priesthood.

And later in your priestly life, you will need close friends, other priests and laypeople, to help you live your vocation to the max. They will encourage you in your weakness and let you know when you are wrong or need to make a change in order to more faithfully follow Christ.

Friends, according to Aristotle, mutually love the other and are both aware of that love; they help each other grow in virtue. Friendship will always require vulnerability, to show myself to the other as I am and to open the doors of my heart. This openness toward others leads me to accept them as they are and to cherish their differences. It is a risk: perhaps some people will betray me and not prove worthy of my trust. But I cannot live a full life without taking this risk.

C. S. Lewis writes in *The Four Loves*:

> To love at all is to be vulnerable. Love anything, and your heart will certainly be wrung and possibly be broken. If you want to make sure of keeping it intact, you must give your heart to no one, not even to an animal. Wrap it carefully round with hobbies and little luxuries; avoid all entanglements; lock it up safe in the casket or coffin of your selfishness. But in that casket—safe, dark, motionless, airless—it will change. It will not be broken; it will become unbreakable, impenetrable, irredeemable. The alternative to tragedy, or at least to the risk of tragedy, is damnation. The only place outside Heaven where you can be perfectly safe from all the dangers and perturbations of love is Hell.[1]

As priests, we need friendships, spiritual friendships. For a priest, a friendship that is not spiritual and ultimately Christ-centered will not have reached its full potential. A friend must help me be my best self, and a priest must be a spiritual man. Any friendship that does not bring me closer to Jesus is not a true friendship even if I enjoy being with the other person.

Going back to *The Lord of the Rings*, would you call Boromir an authentic friend? They've shared many adventures and care for each other, yet he tempts Frodo to take the Ring to Gondor instead of destroying it. He claims Frodo's mission causes him needless suffering.

Boromir tries to get Frodo to take the easy path and when Frodo refuses, tries to take the Ring by force. Friendship must never get in the way of your relationship with Christ or in the way of your mission.

Sure, we are not going to be always discussing the fine points of spiritual progress—at times, we enjoy talking about March Madness or the Super Bowl—just like holiness is not about being in the chapel all day but uniting our will with God's. There are times when you need to take a nap or a vacation!

In friendship, we find some of our greatest consolations; and through our friends, God really shapes and uplifts us. Sharing and hearing how God has worked in my friends' lives has changed my own and encouraged me as I follow Christ. A true friend becomes another Christ in such moments. So often, I have been able to identify with the disciples who had been fleeing to Emmaus: as they run back to Jerusalem after having spent the whole day speaking with Christ about what they kept deepest in their hearts, they say, "Were not our hearts burning [within us] while he spoke to us on the way and opened the scriptures to us?" (Luke 24:32)

Yet where our greatest graces are, there our greatest temptations. The devil will try to take this treasure and twist it into something it was never meant to be. The greatest danger in friendship is that we close in on ourselves and are not open to something greater than that specific relationship. This kind of pseudo-friendship keeps me from growing, from reaching out to others and becoming more like Christ. We become attached to the other person and feel uncomfortable when we are not with them or they are with someone else. C. S. Lewis once wrote that friends stand shoulder to shoulder facing a common object, a shared purpose.[2] True friends always open themselves to a third who shares that same vision.

Can we be friends with everyone? I think we can refer to "friends" as those with whom we have the closest and deepest relationships in our lives. But each relationship with each one of our friends is unique unto itself. Though we will not necessarily be "friends" with everyone, we need to ask ourselves what God wants from each relationship we have. We need to love others as Jesus does, without putting limits on our love if we can help it. Others may put limits, and we respect that. We have our own limits (temperament, culture, prejudices), and we try to reach out in spite of them—only the Heart of Christ can love without reserve. God Himself might put a limit on a relationship so that we learn to love Him more, trusting that God knows what is best for both of us. But on our own initiative, we should never put limits in being open toward deepening a spiritual friendship with another person.

Friendship implies true knowledge of the other, seeing the other (as much as we can or are allowed) as God sees him. We learn to love each person when and how they need to be loved. And through our friends, God will often give us that very same gift.

"Faithful friends are a sturdy shelter; whoever finds one finds a treasure. Faithful friends are beyond price, no amount can balance their worth. Faithful friends are life-saving medicine; those who fear God will find them" (Sir 6:14-16).

Recommended Reading

The Four Loves by C. S. Lewis. Family love, friendship, *eros*, and *agape*—Lewis gives us an excellent investigation into different kinds of relationships.

Love's Sacred Order: The Four Loves Revisited by Erasmo Leiva-Merikakis. He furthers Lewis's reflection on relationships and especially shows how friendship is not purely platonic.

Spiritual Friendship: Darkness and Light by Ronda Chervin. This short work gives excellent criteria for forming a spiritual friendship and its need.

Daring Greatly: How the Courage to Be Vulnerable Transforms the Way We Live, Love, Parent, and Lead by Brené Brown. This book shows the importance of vulnerability with others in order to form deep relationships.

Notes

1. C. S. Lewis, *The Four Loves* (London: Fontana Books, 1973), 111-112.
2. Ibid.

CHAPTER 6
WE WALK DIVERGING PATHS

"Simon Peter said to him, 'Master, where are you going?' Jesus answered [him], 'Where I am going, you cannot follow me now, though you will follow later'" (Jn 13:36). On Holy Thursday, Jesus is about to leave His disciples in obedience to the Father; and in this intimate moment, Jesus wants to communicate to those He loves what He holds in His heart. So He goes on to give His Last Supper discourses.

Communication is a challenge for any relationship. If I want the other person to really know me, he has to understand how I communicate or he will have no idea what I am saying. My words communicate what I carry inside, the deepest parts of my soul. Yet, communication challenges us with an impossibly difficult task. Think about it—when have you ever been able to perfectly communicate with someone you love? Assume that this person knows you well, has spent time with you, has had deep conversations with you, shares many common interests. Most of us have a very short list of this type of person because our hearts are limited; we can love only so much. With these people, above all, we want to go deep, to know them and be known by them.

But it is precisely with these people that we have the longest conversations that never seem to conclude as well as we would like. We talk for hours because we can never quite perfectly communicate with the other, never get them to understand us or to understand them completely. The other remains forever a mystery to me—as I am a mystery for myself. So I am driven to perfectly communicate something I don't even have a clear idea of myself—impossible!

Now, for those of us preparing ourselves to be priests, I suspect that we have a lot more deep relationships than the average person. Consider your own seminary. In the Legion of Christ, I live within a large group of young men who share similar ideals, desires, formation, and world views. We are all in formation for the priesthood and form part of the same spiritual family, called to live the same charism within the Church. Some couples spend years just learning how to communicate with each other, not to mention the later step of coming to the same ideals. We have it handed to us free of charge.

As a seminarian, and later as a priest, we run into a countless number of people who open up their hearts to us, not because of who we are but because they see and seek Christ in us. "No other 'profession,' it seems to me, gives this possibility of knowing the person as he is, in his humanity, rather than in the role he plays in society."[1] It has to have happened to you: you meet someone in the airport or on the street, and they are so excited to see you. In five minutes, they have spilled out their life story, sharing secrets kept from their spouse or friends for decades! And God grants you the privilege to enter into their hearts in a deeper and faster way than the closest people in their lives. Moments like this help us understand what true spiritual fatherhood is.

So, given all these relationships, how can we possibly survive the constant separation? We invest ourselves emotionally and spiritually into people we meet for five minutes on the street; and the moment passes, and we both walk on. We meet with someone for years, helping them on their path toward God and then are assigned a different parish or sent to another country. We form deep friendships with our companions in the seminary, and some will discern it is not their calling; some will finish studies and be sent off to ministry. We have shared joys and struggles, studies and apostolate, received good examples, been helped up after our falls.

Of all these people who pass through our lives, most we will not see again. Our lives are full of separation; and at times, we feel like crying out to Our Lord, *Why? Why the separation, and why does it hurt so much?*

Relationships are meant to last, and it discourages us when they seem to fade away. How can we deal with the separation in our lives as we follow Christ?

We have the coping method used by secular society: memory. In my seminary in Rome, we go to the cemetery on All Soul's Day. Many of the tombstones have a phrase etched in the rock: "*Resterai per sempre nei nostri cuori.*" (You will remain in our hearts forever). Instead of focusing on the loss, we try to remember and be grateful for the time we have had together. We try to freeze the past, keep the memory fresh.

Ed Sheeran's song "Photograph" captures this approach:

We keep this love in a photograph;
We made these memories for ourselves:

Where our eyes are never closing,
Hearts are never broken,
And time's forever frozen, still.

So you can keep me
Inside the pocket of your ripped jeans,
Holding me closer 'til our eyes meet;
You won't ever be alone, wait for me to come home.[2]

Yes, we need to cherish memories of our loved ones, but is that enough? Seems a bit too stoic, and it could lead to imprisonment in the past. I would propose three additional partial answers or intuitions toward one—without pretending anyone can come up with a perfect answer in this life.

First of all, we are able to accept separation because we sincerely seek what is best for the other. A father accepts a certain separation from his family—he needs to work so his family can eat. Parents allow their children to go to school, a separation for the good of their children that will only increase as the children grow and gain more independence. At times, we simply need to let go. If I sincerely seek what is best for the other, I must recognize that their good will can always be found in following God's will: I trust that God will take care of that person better than I ever could. Of course, just because I accept a separation does not mean it is any less painful.

Our second partial answer is that God has given us a very big heart. None of the relationships begun in His name will be lost forever. God gives us a heart for everyone He puts into our lives, an infinitely big heart when we love as we are called to, with Christ's Heart. His Heart bears sufferings too deep for words. Still, because we are part of Christ's Mystical

Body, we are united always to our brothers and sisters through grace, especially when we pray for each other at the Eucharistic Sacrifice.

So, we have these first two answers or solutions for separation, and most of my fellow seminarians have not been satisfied. Separation still hurts, and terribly—I mean, you have to live it, and spiritual explanations or abstract reasoning will change nothing. Granted. But that brings me to the third "answer," which I think is the only one that really satisfies. "I will see you again, and your hearts will rejoice, and no one will take your joy away from you" (Jn 16:22).

Most of us see separation on a purely horizontal level, as a dynamic of loss—we simply have to learn to deal with it. But what if we saw it not as a dynamic of loss but of *waiting*? We have never been able to perfectly communicate with that other person, never gotten them to understand just how much Christ loves them and how much we love them in Christ. But in heaven . . . "At present we see indistinctly, as in a mirror, but then face to face. At present I know partially; then I shall know fully, as I am fully known" (1 Cor 13:12). With God's grace, we are all heading for heaven, our final home. There, all our relationships will be perfect. We will perfectly understand the other and perfectly be understood: perfect communication is perfect communion. We will be together with those we love with absolutely no fear and no possibility of separation: in the communion of saints, all are united in Christ.

Here on earth, all relationships must come to an end: people move away, become bored with each other, die. There, our relationships are forever. We tolerate the smaller separation now in hope of a deeper and more perfect union afterward: the dynamic of waiting. We can accept separation from those we have come to love according to the strength of our hope in heaven.

C. S. Lewis, at the end of his book *The Last Battle*, hints at that indescribable and everlasting joy: everyone from the other Narnia stories is there; and Lucy, Peter, and Edmund will never be sent away from Aslan again.

> And as He spoke He no longer looked to them like a lion; but the things that began to happen after that were so great and beautiful that I cannot write them. And for us this is the end of all the stories, and we can most truly say that they all lived happily ever after. But for them it was only the beginning of the real story. All their life in this world and all their adventures in Narnia had only been the cover and the title page: now at last they were beginning Chapter One of the Great Story which no one on earth has read: which goes on forever: in which every chapter is better than the one before.[3]

Only one relationship has, in itself, the power to last and grow through any crisis, even in spite of death itself. On this journey of life, we are called to form a poor heart, a heart that does not load itself down with things along the path, a heart racing toward heaven. As we are resurrected with Christ, all our relationships are made whole in Him.

"I heard a loud voice from the throne saying, 'Behold, God's dwelling is with the human race. . . . He will wipe every tear from their eyes, and there shall be no more death or mourning, wailing or pain, for the old order has passed away.' The one who sat on the throne said, 'Behold, I make all things new'" (Rev 21:3-5).

Recommended Reading

The Weight of Glory by C. S. Lewis. This is my favorite Lewis essay; on heaven and glory.

Notes

1. Benedict XVI, General Audience, 26 February 2009, http://w2.vatican.va/content/benedict-xvi/en/speeches/2009/february/documents/hf_ben-xvi_spe_20090226_clergy-rome.html (accessed 14 August 2017).
2. "Photograph," by Ed Sheerhan, Johnny McDaid, Jeff Bhasker, 2014.
3. C. S. Lewis, *The Last Battle* (Middlesex: Puffin Books, 1964), 165.

CHAPTER 7
PRAYER'S PURPOSE

The 2016 sci-fi movie *Arrival* tells the story of Louise Banks, a linguist called upon by the government to try and establish communications with one of twelve alien ships that have arrived on different parts of the globe. The aliens allow small groups into their ships and seem to have a form of writing or speaking that no one has so far been able to decipher.

Over several visits, Louise discovers that the aliens have an entirely different concept of language: atemporal. Slowly, she manages to communicate basic words such as "bird" and "human" and moves toward the goal of something more complicated and abstract—what the government is most interested in: "What is your purpose here?"

As their communication improves, she begins to sympathize more and more with the aliens, thus growing in understanding—a virtuous circle. Yet the aliens' way of communication is far more sophisticated and precise than anything humans could have imagined. So, they end up using their "timelessness" to teach Louise their language by showing her the language she has already learned in the future—a kind of revelation, where seeking for the gift and asking for it mean in a certain way that the gift has already been given. Ironically, Louise's encounter with the aliens will lead to a breakdown of communication with her husband and, thus, causes a divorce—lack of communication, lack of intimacy.[1]

Prayer is communication with God—that simple—and leads us to intimacy with Him. It is beyond anything we could work out on our own, and so Eternity must enter into time and reveal Himself to us. Just asking Him to help us pray shows that He has already started to give us that grace. And in prayer, we face the big questions: Who is God? Who are we? What does God want with us? What is His purpose?

I have to admit that my original plan was to read several (more) heavy-duty books on prayer before writing this section so I would be "ready" because sincerely, I am not always faithful to my prayer, and my prayer life is not nearly as deep as it should be with all the graces received in my life. I cannot give you a complete treatise on prayer. (You can find several in the "Recommended Reading" section.) It is beyond my ability and beyond the scope of these reflections. I do want to leave you with a few ideas that will hopefully help you in this crazy adventure of learning how to listen to and speak with God, something far more difficult and beyond our natural ability than talking with aliens.

You Need It

Yes, I know it's obvious. But I still need to remind myself of this simple fact of spiritual life. If my body "forgot" to breathe at night, I would die. Breath is life, and prayer is breath. By now, I have realized that I can trust enough in my own weakness to know that I will not be able to live a faithful and joyful Christian life if I do not pray.

Life flows in ups and downs that frequently follow my fidelity to prayer. When I rely too much on myself and too little on prayer, burnout enters (stage right). As Bishop Ricken writes:

> Burnout stems from a priest's failure to cultivate intimacy with God as the first priority of his priestly existence and is the direct result of the priest giving the substance of his life and person to his work. When the substance of the priest's life and person is given to God, the overflow into priestly and pastoral work is rich and nourishing, and the priest is literally inexhaustible.[2]

Deep prayer leads to deep conversion and deep living. Prayer anchors me in God, centers my heart so I can resist temptations against my vocation. Saint Ignatius's tenth rule for discernment (first week) says that during times of consolation, we need to prepare and strengthen ourselves for moments of desolation and difficulty. Along similar lines, prayer allows me to weather the strongest storms. It will keep me rooted in my ideals:

> Prayer is often difficult because insensitivity to God has become an entrenched attitude. Genuine prayer, because it is true communion with God, keeps expectations high. It prevents that lowering of expectations that often comes with "experience" and that loss of idealism that some look upon as maturity. True prayer nourishes a genuine idealism and does not permit ideals to die in the arena of practical affairs.[3]

Saint Teresa of Calcutta once told a newly-ordained priest that Mass, Rosary, and Liturgy of the Hours each day were not enough for his prayer life because love cannot reduce itself to the bare minimum—on the contrary, it seeks the most possible![4]

Jesus talks about useless servants—they do a lot, but it is not a big deal since they are bound to do it:

> Who among you would say to your servant who has just come in from plowing or tending sheep in the field, "Come here immediately and take your place at table"? Would he not rather say to him, "Prepare something for me to eat. Put on your apron and wait on me while I eat and drink. You may eat and drink when I am finished"? Is he grateful to that servant because he did what was commanded? So should it be with you. When you have done all you have been commanded, say, "We are unprofitable servants; we have done what we were obliged to do" (Lk 17:7-10).

Yet, at the Last Supper, Jesus says that we are no longer servants, but friends—called to love and intimacy!

A wise priest once told us in a conference that the priest's vocation is so radically oriented toward God that he of necessity must become either a saint or a complete disaster—no room for middle ground. It is as if our vocation has given us fish gills in exchange for our lungs so it would be absurd to try and live out of the water. Rather, we should explore the depths of the infinite ocean of God.

Through prayer, God starts to reveal Himself to us, in silence and in mystery. We know that. But the priest, and any person at all, really, must deepen his knowledge and love of God in order to grow in knowledge and love of himself. God holds the secret of my existence in His hand. He knows why

I am here, what I was made for, secrets I have no idea are buried in my heart. So, prayer also gives me my identity.

Dante makes his spiritual journey through hell and purgatory to heaven and his vision of God. The culmination of the vision and the *Divine Comedy* itself, after over 14,200 lines of (prayerful) poetry, tells us that within the Trinity, Dante discovers his own likeness in one of the three Persons. Jesus Christ, God and perfect man, shows me who I truly am called to be.

Souls Need It

You do not need prayer just to keep yourself afloat. A lot of people are riding on your fidelity and on your connection to God. Yes, many people who ask us for prayers live their prayer more faithfully than we do, yet the priest by vocation is intercessor and channel for the transforming grace with which God wants to fill His children.

The Greek word "grace" implies both the gift God wishes to give us and the immense beauty He wants to breathe into us. A priestly intercessor stands between the people and God: gives God's words and grace to the people and offers the people's prayer to God.

We can think of Moses begging God not to destroy Israel after the people had betrayed God and worshipped the golden calf. He pleads and bargains with God, reminding Him all He has done for His people. Moses stands in the breach between God and His people. Later, we have Moses who sustains Israel through his prayer. As long as his hands are upraised in prayer, Israel starts to win the battle. But when he lowers them, the Amalekites have the upper hand. The priest's prayer sustains his people in a way just as real as

Moses's prayer and in the much more important battle for eternal life and sanctity.

The priest must preach God's word to his people, and as Jesus reminds us, "A good person out of the store of goodness in his heart produces good . . . for from the fullness of the heart the mouth speaks" (Lk 6:45). My words will communicate what my heart is full of, what I live and breathe each day and hour, so they had better be full of God. You will not be able to describe or lead others into an experience of God if you are not connected to God!

Finally, a priest must be not only a preacher of prayer but a teacher of it. He must lead others along the path to intimacy with God. While no one can claim a full understanding of how God acts in the lives of souls to draw them to Himself, we hope to have had some experience of it with which to work.

The Apostles first see how Jesus prays and are amazed. Then, comes the plea, "Lord, teach us to pray" (Lk 11:1). How many people approach a priest with this request after having seen him pray his breviary or Rosary? Hopefully, it happens; and hopefully, we are ready to teach them as Jesus did, to introduce them to the Love of our lives.

Intimacy

"Draw near to God, and he will draw near to you" (Jas 4:8).

Prayer leads me into a personal relationship with my God and Creator. It forms my mind and will and heart according to *His* criteria so I can do *His* work as *He* wishes—that is what discernment is all about, and I hope to touch on this more deeply in the next chapter of this book. Prayer helps me find and maintain my purpose in life, to break out of routine and take in the vast horizon of my vocation: I am loved and in love and called to love.

Let's look at the story of *The Little Prince* to try and enter into this idea of intimacy with God. One of the core chapters in the book is where the Little Prince meets the fox, who asks to be tamed.

> "To me, you are still nothing more than a little boy who is just like a hundred thousand other little boys. And I have no need of you. And you, on your part, have no need of me. To you, I am nothing more than a fox like a hundred thousand other foxes. But if you tame me, then we shall need each other. To me, you will be unique in all the world. To you, I shall be unique in all the world."[5]

Here, we get our first aspect of intimacy: uniqueness. There can be no true intimacy with someone who is "just like everyone else," toward whom we feel indifferent. I cannot be indifferent toward God, toward the time I have to give Him in prayer. My fidelity to prayer time is personal—not just "something else I have to do." It is the reason I have life and what I live for!

In a way, each person is as different from another as the race of aliens in *Arrival* is from humans, with their own ways of communicating and understanding and thinking (and loving). So, every priest's relationship with God is unique. God speaks to my heart in ways only I can understand, and I speak with Him as no other person on earth. That is what He loves about me.

My relationship with God requires time, as does any serious relationship. Again, in the words of the fox, "It is the time you have wasted for your rose that makes your rose so important."[6] How much time do I spend with God, really wanting to be with Him? That says much about where my heart is and who God is for me.

Relationships have moments of spontaneity, of surprise and laughter—otherwise, they would be dead! But they also need the consistency and patience of ritual (such as the Liturgy of the Hours) to provide the space in which a relationship can grow. Regularity allows me to prepare my heart for the moment of encounter.

> "It would have been better to come back at the same hour," said the fox. "If, for example, you come at four o'clock in the afternoon, then at three o'clock I shall begin to be happy. I shall feel happier and happier as the hour advances. At four o'clock, I shall already be worrying and jumping about. I shall show you how happy I am! But if you come at just any time, I shall never know at what hour my heart is to be ready to greet you . . . One must observe the proper rites."
>
> "What is a rite?" asked the little prince.
>
> "Those also are actions too often neglected," said the fox. "They are what make one day different from other days, one hour from other hours."[7]

Rites make up any healthy relationship: the family dinner on Sundays, a husband kissing his wife before going to work. The constants in a relationship and in prayer build trust—I know that God will always be there for me, and I form habits of turning to Him and trying to be there for God. There is strength in the ritual and joy in the spontaneity.

A static relationship/prayer life, where I am satisfied with where I am and do not feel the need to change or go deeper, is dead or dying. My relationship with God must grow and bear fruit. There is always more to discover, more reasons to fall in love. And this "ever greater" dynamic of prayer prepares me for heaven, for pure intimacy with God. In the words of Benedict XVI, "God is so great that we will never be finished knowing him. He is always new. [In heaven o]urs is continuous and infinite motion, an ever-new discovery and an ever-new joy."[8]

Recommended Reading

Fire Within: Teresa of Avila, John of the Cross and the Gospel on Prayer by Thomas Dubay, SM. Father Dubay gives us a synthesis of the teaching of Saint Teresa of Ávila and Saint John of the Cross.

Praying the Liturgy of the Hours: A Personal Journey by Timothy M. Gallagher, OMV. This book shows how the author has grown and deepened in his prayer over forty years.

When the Well Runs Dry: Prayer Beyond the Beginnings by Thomas Green, SJ. This book deals with dryness in prayer from an angle combining Saint Teresa of Ávila and Saint Ignatius.

One Thousand Gifts: A Dare to Live Fully Right Where You Are by Ann Voskamp. This poetical prose helps deepen the importance of thanksgiving for our spiritual lives.

Crazy Love: Overwhelmed by a Relentless God by Francis Chan. There are some great ideas here about the need to fall madly in love with God.

NOTES

1. *Arrival.* Directed by Denis Villeneuv. Hollywood, CA: Paramount Pictures, 2016.

2. David L. Ricken, *Be Thou My Vision* (Omaha: IPF Publications, 2009), 24.

3. Ibid., 89.

4. "Cardinal Comastri Recounts How Mother Teresa Saved His Priesthood," *Catholic News Agency* (August 26, 2010), https://www.catholicnewsagency.com/news/20681/cardinal-comastri-recounts-how-mother-teresa-saved-his-priesthood.

5. Antoine de Saint-Exupéry, *The Little Prince* (New York: Reynal and Hitchcock, 1943), 66.

6. Ibid., 72.

7. Ibid., 67-68.

8. Benedict XVI, *Ultime Conversazioni*, Garzanti, Milano 2016, 28. The translation is mine from the Italian: "Dio è tanto grande che noi non finiamo mai di conoscerlo. È sempre nuovo. Il nostro è un moto continuo e infinito, una scoperta e una gioia sempre nuove."

CHAPTER 8
DISCERNING THE CALL

Even children's stories can help us enter into some of the deepest and most important life issues. In the movie *Rise of The Guardians*, the Man in the Moon has gathered an odd assortment of characters to protect children. Santa leads the Guardians; the Tooth Fairy protects memory; the Easter Bunny gives hope; and Sandman, peace. (I know, a pretty wacky story premise, but the movie is superb.)[1]

Jack Frost finds himself brought into being by the Man in the Moon—for what purpose, he has no idea. The Man in the Moon eventually tells the guardians of the children that Jack Frost has been chosen to be one of them. Yet, he has no idea who he is or what he could protect in a child.

At one point, Santa asks him, "Who are you, Jack Frost? What is your center?" Jack does not understand, so Santa takes a Russian doll of Santa. The first doll is fierce, the one inside that jolly, then mysterious, fearless, caring . . . and at his core is a child with eyes of wonder. Wonder is Santa's center, his mission in the world. Only after Jack Frost discovers his center can he freely embrace and fulfill his mission.

Who am I? For what was I put on earth? Vocational discernment helps us discover what God has planned for our lives; and through it, we discover our identity, who we are in the innermost core of our being. The priesthood is beautiful and awesome—when I say "awesome," I mean inspiring awe and reverence before something beyond the human. (From what I have experienced so far of the call, I cannot wait to live its fullness after ordination!)

A simple definition of discernment could be learning to listen to God. Now, maybe you are the exception; but for most of us, God usually does not appear in a dream or vision. He does not spell things out and hand us the brochure with the diocesan vocation director's contact information or the address of a religious congregation. We need to become men of discernment: to pick up the subtle messages God sends us that often break beyond our preconceived ideas and expectations.

Why discern your vocation? The absolute worst-case scenario would be to receive priestly ordination and then find out that it was not for you; unless God intervenes with some very special grace (hopefully, this happens more often than not . . .), it would mean either leaving the priesthood or living a restricting and frustrated life that does not let you be who you were called to be.

What has God created me for? The question is essential. It is urgent, and there is danger in delaying it. Why? The rest of your life depends on it! And if God has something else planned for you, you will want to get started right away.

I have known seminarians who have ignored or never seriously asked themselves the vocational question until a year or two before ordination, and the more they have put it off, the harder it becomes to face. But the problem does not go away. It grows. And no one can deny the hurt in discovering after much work and study that you do not have a priestly vocation. I mean, you put years, a decade of your life, into something only to have it all collapse? That is how it can seem. The pain of finding out that this is not your path is not something I have experienced myself. But God has placed me in situations where I have been able to accompany many of my brothers who have come to this realization. Very difficult, but so worthwhile.

For me, there are few better examples of courage than that shown by a young man who accepts God's call to lay life after having begun the path toward the priesthood, who trusts that God—who has walked with him thus far—will not abandon him now. It is the faith of Abraham who leaves everything he had planned and accumulated during his life to follow God to the promised land. The courage of such individuals inspires me and gives me strength to live out my own calling. In this way, we strengthen each other.

Motivation

Before diving into discernment proper, we need to consider some aspects on a more human level. First of all, I need to know why I am here, why I joined the seminary. What motivates me? There could be negative motivations that I will have to purify or overcome: escaping the world; because my family wants it; to get attention . . . And there are positive motivations (many of which also have to be purified): to get a good education; to help other people overcome poverty or difficult family situations, love for souls, esteem for the priesthood, love for Christ, etc.

We will not have one single motivation in following this vocation, but I need to make sure that my deepest motivations are valid. I need to take the time to know myself and go deep into what I really want, to be sincere in my motivations before myself and before God. You might discover that you do not have the best of motivations at first, but that's okay because motivations can evolve and deepen.

One of my friends in seminary (we are still friends) eventually discerned, after quite a while, that the priesthood in my congregation was not his calling. He had wanted to follow Jesus completely and had seen the priestly vocation as the most generous path, the path leading to greatest perfection and closeness to Our Lord. He longed for holiness. At the same time, he had a vision of marriage as somehow "less" than the priesthood, that it was the less generous option. When he realized God was calling him to lay life, he had to recognize that he was not being called to be less holy because of that. He had to learn that marriage is a beautiful calling and a deeply overwhelming mystery of beauty and adventure.

To be able to fully accept and live out your vocation, you need to understand and meditate on the beauty of marriage. First of all, you need to know what you are giving up in order to be able to make the sacrifice. And then, as a priest, you will need to help married couples on their path to holiness. The priestly vocation is a gift and a sacrifice—you need to make sure that you receive the gift and make the sacrifice for the right reasons.

Compatibility

Staying on a human and rational level, the question of compatibility enters into discernment. It is a double-ended question: between me and the diocese or congregation where I think God is calling me. Just like a valid marriage, a priestly vocation requires mutual consent. Both of us need to feel that we belong together in the same family.

There are certain virtues I will need and bad habits to have avoided completely or overcome. Can I get along with others? Do I know how to listen to others and how to obey? This will affect my relationship with my parishioners and with my bishop or superior. Do I have a habit of purity? A persistent addiction to pornography would be a serious obstacle for the priesthood. Do I have the intelligence needed to complete the studies for the priesthood and to be able to explain the faith to others? Is my psychology and temperament compatible with the priestly vocation? If I do not like to stay in one place for long, it could be a problem if later, I am assigned to the same parish for six years or more.

Many of these personality traits have nothing to do with being "better" or "worse." I think every priest has met many people who have nowhere near his theological preparation yet have a better religious sense and a deeper knowledge of the things of God than he does. Some different personality traits may be required in different groups or dioceses. For example, I am a member of an international congregation that could send me across the globe for my ministry. So I need a minimal openness to other cultures because I will either end up living in another culture myself or living in the same community with those of different cultures.

The one thing compatibility is *not*: a question of being strong or stubborn or generous or good enough to "make it" in the priestly vocation. You have probably seen the baby toy consisting of a plastic box with different-shaped holes and the different blocks the kid has to slide through them. It's not that the cylinder is better than the block, but if you try to force the block through the circular opening, it will simply not enter, or it will break. God has given us all different graces in order to follow Him. He calls us all to holiness, to intimacy with Him. And He gives us different graces and traits to get there. The presence or lack of the necessary compatibility allows us to discern on a human level the possibility of a vocation.

Standing before God

Taking into account all of the above, we enter into the supernatural. This is actually where vocation discernment must start and end, before seeing your motivations and compatibility—they are seen and analyzed within and with a view toward understanding what God has to say about your life. This happens through prayer.

Before making lists of pros and cons or comparing one way of life with another, you need to foster a deep relationship with Jesus, a deep prayer life. God appeared and spoke to Elijah on the mountain in the form of a soft breeze—not in the earthquake, fire, or wild wind (see 1 Kings 19:11-12). Create pools of silence in your life where you can hear the whispers of God's voice. Learn to listen. Learn to relate with Him. God wants to reveal Himself and His plan to you, so ask Him to! "And the one who searches hearts knows what is the intention of the Spirit because it intercedes for the holy ones according to God's will" (Rm 8:27).

Discernment requires sincerity with yourself and with God—when you ask Him to show you His will, you need to mean it! That means being open to whatever He shows you, whatever path He may lead you along, not waiting for a confirmation of what you have already decided on your own.

How can you be completely open? I think the key may be understanding that God wants you to be happy—fully, completely, overwhelmingly happy. That is what He made you for. God does not want you to simply do the hardest thing possible, though He may ask hard things of you. He does not want you to suffer, though He may permit it in order to allow you to grow closer to Him. Whatever He asks or allows, He has your happiness and best interests at heart. He is your Father. Discovering your vocation will be discovering the deepest desires of your heart, longings you were perhaps unaware of before. "The kingdom of heaven is like a treasure buried in a field, which a person finds and hides again, and out of joy goes and sells all that he has and buys that field" (Mt 13:44).

Some Signs

I am going to finish with some practical signs for discernment. These go beyond the rational and human signs we saw above, which should be integrated into your prayer.

The first sign is peace in prayer, peace that is real, deep, and not passing. You pray about certain decisions and over time, realize that God gives an overwhelming calm—not passivity, but assurance. It does not come from human security or calculations but from prayer and trust. Saint Ignatius says that we should never make a decision in a time of turmoil or distress. A lack of peace means that you should keep praying and discerning. Maybe you are not quite where God wants you yet.

The second sign is happiness. This is very similar to the first, but on a vocational level, it means making the "click" and realizing, "Hey! I could spend the rest of my life like this. This is what I was made for."

The third sign is humility. This means that you are open to placing what you have discerned and think God is asking of you before the Church. You are not your own best judge and need a good spiritual director (which every seminary should have) to guide you through your feelings and perceptions of God.

This chapter touches on some of discernment's basic elements, but you can go so much deeper into this theme! You should definitely see some of the books suggested below for a more detailed discussion. This is your life.

Recommended Reading

Discerning the Will of God: An Ignatian Guide to Christian Decision Making by Timothy Gallagher, OMV. This is a practical book on Ignatius's discernment methods—very helpful and straightforward. Father Gallagher has two other excellent books on the topic, but this one is principally on vocational discernment.

Authenticity: A Biblical Theology of Discernment by Thomas Dubay, SM. As always, Father Dubay challenges the reader deeply. He comments on discernment criteria found in the Scriptures.

Weeds Among the Wheat by Thomas H. Green, SJ. An excellent summary of Ignatian spirituality, the book touches on both general discernment (as in the Timothy Gallagher book above) and more specific day-to-day discernment (like the Timothy Gallagher books mentioned later).

NOTES

1. *Rise of the Guardians.* Directed by Peter Ramsey. Glendale, CA: Dreamworks Animation, 2012.

Chapter 9
Listen: In the Silence, for the Silence

The prophet Elijah stunned all Israel when he proclaimed a drought throughout the land. He swept the people into his wake after calling down fire from heaven and slaughtering the four hundred fifty prophets of Baal one by one: a mighty man of action, a leader blessed by God and called to work wonders.

Yet immediately after, Elijah must flee for his life; and, alone in the desert, he begins to doubt God and his calling: "I have been most zealous for the Lord, the God of hosts, but the Israelites have forsaken your covenant. They have destroyed your altars and murdered your prophets by the sword. I alone remain, and they seek to take my life" (1 Kgs 19:10). He travels alone until he reaches Mount Horeb. The man of God must search for God, and God is found only in silence:

> There was a strong and violent wind rending the mountains and crushing rocks before the Lord—but the Lord was not in the wind; after the wind, an earthquake—but the Lord was not in the earthquake; after the

> earthquake, fire—but the Lord was not in the fire; after the fire, a light silent sound (1 Kgs 19:11-12).

There, in the silence, Elijah discovers God. He discovers himself. And he is given his mission.

The great mystics present God to us as the Unknown. Saint Augustine's famous phrase sums it up: *si comprehendis, non est Deus*—if you think you know God, you are way off! God is beyond our mind's capacity, so any idea we form of God has to fall short. I recently ran across these lines from Saint Gregory of Nyssa:

> It is not in the nature of what is unenclosed to be grasped. But every desire for the Good which is attracted to that ascent constantly expands as one progresses in pressing on to the Good. This truly is the vision of God: never to be satisfied in the desire to see him. But one must always, by looking at what he can see, rekindle his desire to see more. Thus, no limit would interrupt growth in the ascent to God, since no limit to the Good can be found nor is the increasing of desire for the Good brought to an end because it is satisfied.[1]

Saint Gregory gives us the figure of Moses, who understands something of God, but at once, leaves behind what he understands, since it is only an imperfect image, to deepen in his understanding in what no one could ever understand.

No concept could ever contain God. So in consequence, no words could ever convey who God is—only one unpronounceable Word from the mouth of God Himself. So, we must become men of silence who do not try to contain God in our thoughts or words, who listen for the Word.

Listen to God

We have many challenges to silence embedded in our culture and surroundings. Today, most people fear silence and interiority. What if they were to find God in it? Or worse—what if they were to find themselves? We have the internet constantly flinging information and links and promotions and videos and news flashes . . . We need to have music playing all the time, or at least some kind of noise in the background. We get nervous if we leave our phone behind. We tend to say anything that comes into our head, creating useless noise for others: blogs, the comment box, tweets, texts, phone calls. And when was the last time you actually made eye contact during a conversation?

You need to be aware of the culture surrounding you and embrace all the healthy possibilities it offers in communication; but at the same time, you must deliberately work to become a man of silence. Otherwise, it will not happen.

"For when peaceful stillness encompassed everything and the night in its swift course was half spent, Your all-powerful word from heaven's royal throne leapt into the doomed land" (Ws 18:14-15). Jesus Christ, the Word of God, enters the world in silence, thanks to the silence of Mary who is able to listen to God's messenger; thanks to the Holy Spirit, the great Unknown, who always works in silence.

The Holy Spirit works your soul and, little by little, is molding you into Christ. He is the only one who can do it, so you have to listen to Him. He shapes, chisels (it can hurt!), and polishes in order to give you true life. He Himself is Life, and you have to breathe Him if you hope to be His instrument in giving Life to others.

I hear nothing! Yet the Word is too immense for your ears. *I understand nothing!* Then you have understood what is most important.

Silence creates a space where you can learn how to listen and how to pray. Little by little, you should develop an intuition for the things of God, a sixth sense that leads you beyond simple reasoning and onto a supernatural plane. Silence allows God to be God, beyond what you can understand. It is God's language where He whispers to you your identity and your mission.

We have already discussed vocational discernment—in silence, you learn day-to-day discernment: how to live and how to guide others. You learn to live seeking to love God in all things as He wants to be loved. You learn how God wants to love you and seeks to guide you. You listen to your own heart and within it, find His voice.

Mel Gibson's World War II movie *Hacksaw Ridge* tells a true story. Andrew Garfield plays Desmond Doss, a conscientious objector who joins the army as a medic and is sent to the Pacific. In a desperate moment, the American troops are being pushed back off a ridge by the Japanese. Desmond has just had a friend die in his arms and desperately turns to God amid the bullets and explosions: "What is it you want of me? I don't understand. I can't hear you!"

Then, a wounded soldier screams in pain from where the American troops had retreated. And Desmond hears; he understands what God is asking of him and responds, "Alright." He turns back toward the field of battle and ends up single-handedly rescuing over seventy-five wounded soldiers. Desmond did not hear God . . . yet he understood.[2]

Listen to Others

This listening to God will bring you to discover His plans, will reveal what you must do to serve others and fulfill your mission. A man of silence becomes a refuge for souls, an oasis in a world of noise that invites people to go deeper.

The French writer Georges Bernanos puts in the mouth of a simple and saintly country priest:

> Keep silent, what a strange expression! Silence keeps us . . . My inner quiet—blessed by God—has never really isolated me. I feel all human-kind can enter, and I receive them thus only at the threshold of my home. I feel they do come to me, in spite of themselves. Alas, mine is but a very precarious shelter. But I imagine the quiet of some souls is like a vast refuge. Sinners at the end of their tether can creep in and rest, and leave comforted, forgetting the great invisible temple where they lay down their burden for a while.[3]

Your having listened to God will help you listen to others, especially in spiritual direction and in Confession. When leading people to God, you first listen and try to understand what they are saying and where they are. Only then can you help them grow.

Listening to others means, first of all, being there. Completely. God invites them to an exclusive relationship with Himself, and you can reflect that by an exclusive attention given to them. So, you resist other interruptions, doing something on the computer or your cell phone. You need to *be* there.

Step number two: be quiet. Just listen so you can understand the "what." We men like to try and fix things, to give the perfect answer, when often, people just need someone to listen. To guide another, it cannot be about what you *think* he is saying, but *what* he is saying. "Know this, my dear brothers: everyone should be quick to hear, slow to speak" (Jas 1:19).

Finally, discover the "why" behind the "what": their motivations. Sometimes people are unaware of them. As one wise priest once told me, "It's never about what it's about!" But more than the spiritual director's "discovery," it is about helping the person discover for himself what he holds in his heart of hearts. Especially here, we ask the Holy Spirit to come and enlighten us to understand this person before us. Only He can see the truth of every heart because no one loves that person as He does. So ask the Holy Spirit for help. He wants to give it.

Teach Others to Listen

The "solution" lies here and not in anything you can think up on your own! A good spiritual guide gives people the tools, the principles they need in order to enter into relationship with God and learn to hear His voice. He accompanies them, and together, they both seek light to discover what God is asking. You will have to lead souls to prayer, to a sacramental life, to vocational discernment and to apostleship. Guiding souls means helping free them for God.

Though we already touched on discernment previously, I would like to share with you two paradigms that have helped me in my day-to-day discernment. First, everything that happens, God either wants or allows. So, when bad things happen, well, sure, God did not want them to happen. But when he allows these things, it is always for the greater good. Now, this can sound pretty philosophical or even a bit foolish.

Who am I to point out the "reason" for a child starving in Africa or a woman forced into prostitution on the streets of Rome? No one. Yet, this conviction of God wanting or allowing comes as a fruit of a deep supernatural trust. I know who God is, and I cannot doubt His goodness. And the evil in this world has pierced His Heart where it has only touched mine; and where rivers of salt have run down my cheeks, His tears have filled ocean upon countless ocean. I cannot explain the why of evil. God's answer is in His silence.

The other paradigm is the "discernment triangle" of grace-cross-temptation. This explanation I owe to one of my spiritual directors, a priest who has taught me so much about seeking and listening for God. The idea is that everything that happens to you is usually classified as a grace, a cross, or a temptation; when you recognize one of these present in your life, your task is to discern the other two. Otherwise, you risk living the moment or situation according to your first reaction and not opening up to how God might want to work in you.

So, you find yourself in a moment of special grace and consolation in prayer. What does the Cross have to do with that? Perhaps God is preparing you for a moment of difficulty—Ignatian wisdom tells us that in moments of consolation, we should prepare for desolation. Maybe God is using you to sustain another person in their suffering. Maybe He is about to ask you to grow in intimacy with Him, implying a difficult step in generosity. And as for the temptation, how might you be tempted to not take advantage of this grace? That is what you have to discern. In a moment of temptation, you have to discern "where is the grace?" What good does God want me to get out of this moment? How is He strengthening me, leading me? What is the specific cross I am being asked to bear right now?

In a moment of cross and suffering, again, you have to discern "where is God here?" How is He uniting me to His redemptive sacrifice? What is the temptation? How might I try to "[come] down from the cross" and save myself (see Mk 15:30), to not use this pain to draw nearer to Our Lord?

Become a man who listens to God. Silence matters not so much as an absence of noise, but as an active listening to God and as the way in which God speaks to us.

Recommended Reading

He Leadeth Me: An Extraordinary Testament of Faith by Walter Ciszek, SJ. This book shows us discernment in practice as Father Ciszek shows how he discovered and was transformed by God's providence leading him through his captivity in Russia.

Seeking Spiritual Direction: How to Grow the Divine Life Within by Thomas Dubay, SM. Father Dubay lists attitudes and recommendations for someone receiving and giving spiritual direction.

Discernment of Spirits: An Ignatian Guide for Everyday Living by Timothy Gallagher, OMV. This is an in-depth analysis of Ignatius's rules for discernment from the first week of his *Spiritual Exercises.*

Spiritual Consolation: An Ignatian Guide for Greater Discernment of Spirits by Timothy Gallagher, OMV. This is an in-depth analysis of Ignatius's rules for discernment from the second week of the *Spiritual Exercises.*

The Power of Silence: Against the Dictatorship of Noise by Robert Cardinal Sarah. Silence is essential in order to become men of God.

Forming Intentional Disciples: The Path to Knowing and Following Jesus by Sherry A. Weddell. She outlines how to form laity to live the fullness of their vocations in a relationship with Christ that translates into apostolate, within the specific context of the parish.

NOTES

1. Gregory of Nyssa, *The Life of Moses*, trans. Eng. A. Malherbe & E. Ferguson (Mahwah, NJ: Paulist Press, 1978), 116 (nn.238-239).
2. *Hacksaw Ridge*. Directed by Mel Gibson. Santa Monica, CA: Summit Entertainment, 2016.
3. Georges Bernanos, *The Diary of a Country Priest* (Lebanon, IN: Da Capo Press, 2002), 259-260.

Chapter 10
A Mother of Many Sons

Whenever I start talking about Mary, I feel like I want to say so much, yet I often find myself without words. I guess everything I want to say centers around one thought: she is my mother. (Fine. She's yours too. I can share.)

God's Mother and Mine: Core Attitudes

When we look at Mary's faith, at once we think about her *fiat*, her version of "thy will be done." When the angel destroys her expectations and shows her God's plan, she immediately says yes without understanding all of what that yes means. When a mother finds out she is pregnant, she does not know if her child will survive childhood, if he will be popular, handsome, or successful. She does not know if he has Downs Syndrome or a cleft lip. Yet she accepts him; she says yes to her child. And this is Mary's commitment, not only at Nazareth but also at Calvary. Her Son asked her to be our mother as well, to take the whole world into her arms, to care for each and every one of us just as she cared for Him. Right at that moment, in silent assent, Mary committed to you. She accepted your little life and took you into her family.

As a consequence of the above, Mary tries to teach you faith—faith when you cannot see God, when you are not sure if He even exists or if He cares. She wants to take you by the hand and guide you along your journey. God may call you toward Calvary, but she will be with you every step of the way. She points out the light in midst of darkness; and in her shining eyes, you will be able to receive the love of someone who has looked on God.

Mary shows you the meaning of hope. At the darkest moment in her life, she stays standing. Where does she get her strength? Obviously, God holds her up, but I think much of her strength also came from contemplating the past, treasuring what God had done in her heart. And in her heart, she prayed over these memories and formed her convictions that for her became anchors amid the storm. God had worked wonders of love in her life before—He would not abandon her now. In the words of Pope Francis:

> Let us never forget that progressing in faith is never merely a sheer act of the will to believe more strongly from now on; it is also an exercise of returning with our memory to fundamental graces. It is possible to "progress by going backwards", by searching out once again the treasures and experiences that have been forgotten but which nevertheless very often contain keys for understanding the present. This is truly a "revolutionary" thing: to go back to our roots. The clearer our memory of the past, the clearer the future appears to us, because in this way we can see the road that is really new and distinguish it from the roads that have already been taken but that led us nowhere.[1]

And just like Mary never gave up hope in God or in her Son, she never, ever gives up hope in you.

One of the memories that has given foundation to my whole spiritual life happened during my novitiate in Dublin, Ireland. Now, the chapel in our novitiate was very small, so we would go to confession in one of the rooms close by. Everyone waiting for Confession would be at the back of the chapel (usually during our community night prayers) while the next person in line would wait in the hall outside where there was a little bench in front of a statue of Mary.

It was August 23, 2004—I had to go to Confession and was very nervous. I was the last one in line that night, and I found myself sitting on that bench with the wheels in my head spinning: *How can I tell this to Father so I actually say it but so that he doesn't understand what I mean?* (A very interesting question for hermeneutics and sacramental theology, but that is getting off topic.) I pretty much had my phrasing set when the door to the confessional opened. I stood up, and in that moment, someone intoned the final hymn before going to bed: the *Salve Regina* (Hail, Holy Queen). I do not know why or how, but all my plans were washed away; and in that confession, what was really in my heart came tumbling out. That experience is something I have come back to again and again in prayer over the years, and I am convinced that in that moment, Mary saved my vocation.

Mary teaches you to love. Her life was a complete gift to Jesus, and she wants to make it a complete gift to you as well, in the big things and in the details you will not notice until heaven. Mothers give themselves to their children and find their happiness in their children's happiness—just because they are mothers.

So it does not matter what you have done or how you might have distanced yourself from Mary. Her arms are always waiting: whether it is to receive a broken and bleeding body from the Cross or to welcome her Son with joy on Easter Sunday.

Mother of Priests: How She Forms Jesus (and Us!)

When we talk about Jesus's humanity, we need to remember that He got it all from her—literally everything! She gives Him His Body, carries that little baby God in her womb. And as a newborn, He is so helpless He cannot survive without her. He needs her for nourishment, for warmth and love, to change His diapers or give Him a bath. Her arms are where the toddler Jesus runs to cry if He has bloodied His knee or is feeling sad. And as He gets older, she teaches Him table manners, how to greet other adults, and how to clean up around the house. Along with Joseph, Mary teaches Jesus how to love within a family. From her, Jesus learns the value of little acts of kindness or a quick smile when their eyes meet. The Gospels show us Mary's style of love, never putting herself at the center.

God asks her to change all her life plans. She says yes to the angel. She hears she is to be the Mother of God and that Elizabeth is to give birth. She rushes to serve her cousin. Jesus is lost in Jerusalem. She searches three days straight. Jesus grows up having never made her life easier by a miracle. She asks Him to take care of wine shortage at someone else's party. Jesus calls her "woman" instead of mother. She says to do "whatever He tells you" (Jn 2:5). He leaves home to preach the Kingdom. She lets him go freely. He takes up His Cross upon His tortured back. She accepts and follows in His footsteps. He asks her to love John as she had loved Him. She accepts once more.

Mary teaches Jesus the value of silence and how to pray. As she guarded all the graces she received in her heart in solitude with God, so we see Jesus later on looking for time to be alone with His Father, even and especially in the most difficult moments of His life. Mary found God in the simple things, and so we see Jesus using simple examples from everyday life in His preaching. She must have taught Jesus to find God in creation, to make a prayer of each sparrow in the air or flower of the field. She says "*fiat*"; He says, "Thy will be done."

Mary did not keep Jesus for herself, did not keep Him from Calvary. She let Him leave home to begin His public life; and from that moment on, she loved Him especially through her hiddenness, her life lived in obedience. At the foot of the Cross, she stands there for Him. She does not understand God's ways, so she prays. Her years of contemplation and silence give her the strength to accept both the fate of her Son and becoming mother of us all.

And just as Mary taught Jesus to love and to pray, she taught the Apostles in the upper room as they waited for the Holy Spirit. And after they had left to sow the seed of faith among all nations, we have no word of her; but surely, she supported them in prayer and silence as she had done before with Jesus.

This is who Mary wants to be for you, how she wants to form your heart.

How Jesus Treats His Mother

We also need to learn from Jesus how to treat His mother. Take a look at Jesus's obedience and His intimacy with her. After the finding in the Temple, Luke tells us that "He went down with them and came to Nazareth, and was obedient to them" (Lk 2:51). So we know that Jesus obeyed her. But this obedience probably was not so much in the big things as in the little ones of everyday life—otherwise, Luke probably would have told us! Jesus obeyed, helping Mary in simple tasks, studying and growing in virtue. Hidden obedience. And in heaven, Jesus crowns her Queen. She intercedes before Him, and He still listens to her, still chooses obedience!

Then we have their intimacy. Outside of the Trinity, there is no relationship more intimate. In Luke, Jesus shows how well He understands who Mary is and her true greatness, what places her so close to His Heart: "While he was speaking, a woman from the crowd called out and said to him, 'Blessed is the womb that carried you and the breasts at which you nursed.' He replied, 'Rather, blessed are those who hear the word of God and observe it'" (Lk 11:27-28).

Through His whole life, Jesus is known as son of Mary.[2] Jesus accepted that title and wanted it to be transmitted to us in the Bible. And, of course, we have the tradition that Jesus first appeared to Mary on Easter Sunday. I think the Assumption gives us the crowning moment of intimacy between Jesus and His mother. For Jesus, everything about His mother is precious, and He cannot wait to take her, body and soul, into heaven to be with Him!

So learn from Mary. Trust her. Love her. Let Mary take your hand (especially in the Rosary!) and guide you in Jesus's footsteps.

Bride of the Holy Spirit,
obtain for us the inestimable gift
of transformation in Christ.
Through the same power of the Spirit that
overshadowed you,
making you the Mother of the Saviour,
help us to bring Christ your Son
to birth in ourselves too.
May the Church
be thus renewed by priests who are holy,
priests transfigured by the grace of him
who makes all things new.
. . .
Let your presence cause new blooms to burst forth
in the desert of our loneliness,
let it cause the sun to shine on our darkness,
let it restore calm after the tempest,
so that all mankind shall see the salvation
of the Lord,
who has the name and the face of Jesus,
who is reflected in our hearts,
for ever united to yours!

Amen![3]

Recommended Reading

A Woman Wrapped in Silence by John Lynch. This book of free-verse poetry must be read slowly. It helps as a composition of place for the Gospel scenes in Mary's life.

33 Days to Morning Glory: A Do-It-Yourself Retreat in Preparation for Marian Consecration by Michael Gaitley, MIC. A do-it-yourself retreat using Saint Louis de Montfort, Saint Therese of Lisieux, Saint John Paul II, and Mother Teresa.

The World's First Love: Mary, Mother of God by Fulton Sheen. This is a classic must-read book on Marian spirituality.

The Silence of Mary by Ignacio Larrañaga. These interesting reflections on Mary help us enter her interior treasuring of God's grace in her heart.

My Ideal: Jesus, Son of Mary by Emile Neubert, SM. Saint Maximilian Kolbe loved this book!

NOTES

1. Francis, Address to the Parish Priests of the Diocese of Rome, 2 March 2017, https://w2.vatican.va/content/francesco/en/speeches/2017/march/documents/papa-francesco_20170302_parroci-roma.html (accessed 14 May 2017).
2. See Mark 6:3.
3. Benedict XVI, "Act of Entrustment and Consecration of Priests to the Immaculate Heart of Mary, 12 May 2010," accessed 16 August 2017, http://w2.vatican.va/content/benedict-xvi/en/prayers/documents/hf_ben-xvi_20100512_affidamento-fatima.html.

CHAPTER 11
ONE FATHER

Every man longs for fruitfulness, to make a mark on the world and on history. No one really wants only comfort, just to be left alone, unless they have been terribly wounded and have taken refuge in cynicism. Greatness calls us, and we long to matter—of course, being remembered in gratitude would be ideal, but for some, better to be remembered with fear and hatred than holding no place at all in memory.

Jesus calls you to bear fruit in your priesthood—not fruit that withers after a few decades or even centuries, but fruit that lasts.[1] Beyond the rise and fall of empires and civilizations, beyond all history: fruit for eternity! The life God wills to transmit through you is the fullness of life, cosmic and eternal. Spiritual fatherhood.

God is Father, as opposed to merely being a master. He is Shepherd of the Flock, not a hired hand; a Father who gives to His children, not a master who takes; a Father who raises His children to freedom, not one who condemns them to servile and lasting repetitiveness. God is Father: "the Lord, your God, carried you, as one carries his own child, all along your journey" (Dt 1:31).

Now me, I love kids. I love holding a little baby in my arms (as long as it is not crying!) and making it laugh by speaking jumbled baby gibberish that we both understand perfectly as he laughs and pulls on my finger. I love discussing serious matters with five-year-olds: the dragons hidden in the sandbox or why Mister Strawhead, a very important toy, likes catfish with his pancakes. I love teasing kids by pretending to shake their hands and laughing when they are not quite fast enough to catch mine. So when I think about what it means to be a dad, my heart explodes with wonder and longing. To love and raise, to guard and defend, to teach and to give dignity. My own dad did all that for me, taught me what it meant to be a man and father, and in the process, made himself my hero.

How do you know if a kid will grow up to be a good father? It starts with his relationship with his dad. And a priest? Look at his relationship with the Father. You can best prepare by being a good son, by watching your dad do everything and trying to do it like he would. No matter your relationship with your father, we all need to learn to be fathers from God: you will be a father because He has shared His fatherhood with you. So let us take a moment to learn how to be a father from God Himself—how is God my father, and what does He do for me? In order to become a father, I must first learn to be a son.

> Faith in my fatherhood will be the path of healing for many, who, like you, were kept from growing up in freedom and joy beneath the gaze of their father. I want to banish fear from your life. I want you to feel loved and surrounded by My presence as *FATHER*—a presence that supports you, that will not hold you back

from becoming the man that I have always wanted you to be—a presence that will allow you, in turn, to become a father, a father in My image, a father as My Jesus was fully a father in the midst of His disciples. They discovered My fatherhood in His countenance. They sensed it in drawing close to His Heart; they saw it at work in the signs of mercy and of power that He worked in My Name.

It must be so for you. Be the image of My fatherhood. By means of the fatherly love that I shall place in your heart, be My instrument for the healing of many who did not know what it is to be loved by a father.[2]

Heart of a Son

Growth as a son overcomes the deepest doubts in a man's heart: *Who am I? Who is God?* How can we arrive at Saint Paul's conclusion: "You received a spirit of adoption, through which we cry, 'Abba, Father!'" (Rom 8:15)? God wants an intimate relationship with you, His beloved son.

First of all, how does the Father see you? Well, we know that He sees everything—nothing is hidden from Him. "When you pray, go to your inner room, close the door, and pray to your Father in secret. And your Father who sees in secret will repay you" (Mt 6:6). Yes, He knows everything, and that would be pretty discouraging if that were all there were to God's seeing us. I mean, we all know how weak and full of faults we are, and if there is no chance of making a good first impression, what chance is there?

We can take our cue from the book of Hosea to go deeper into how the Father sees us. The prophet portrays God as a Father holding His Son, Israel, fast by the hand as

He takes His first few tottering steps. But God is remembering this fact after His Son has grown up and rebelled against Him!

> When Israel was a child I loved him, out of Egypt I called my son. The more I called them, the farther they went from me, sacrificing to the Baals and burning incense to idols. Yet it was I who taught Ephraim to walk, who took them in my arms; but they did not know that I cared for them. I drew them with human cords, with bands of love; I fostered them like those who raise an infant to their cheeks; I bent down to feed them (Hos 11:1-4).

When God sees you in your sinful weakness, He cannot help but remember how much He has loved and cared for you. And in spite of your sin—in the case of Israel, repeated and conscientious rejection of their Father as they placed their trust in idols—there is never a moment when you stop being His child. No matter how your father on earth saw you or treated you, God is your true father. He delights in you! And though you might be uncertain about the future of your relationship with God, He never hesitates for a moment. There is no way He is going to give up on you. Continuing with Hosea, right after God says, "How could I give you up, Ephraim, or deliver you up, Israel? . . . . My heart is overwhelmed, my pity is stirred" (Hos 11:8).

Your Father sees you. He has dreams for you. He believes in you. When God the Father sent Jesus into the world, He had Jesus come as a little baby. Who can be afraid of a baby, right? Jesus in that manger is weak and helpless. Our most natural reaction before any baby is to care for it. Its weakness does not evoke contempt but tenderness, not indifference but constant attention.

Well, it turns out God took a page from humanity's book—that is how He sees you in your weakness and sin, just as you see Jesus wrapped warm in swaddling clothes and Mary's arms. God does not reject you but takes pity and longs even more to draw you to Himself.

Once you meditate on how the Father sees you, the next question comes naturally: how does He want you to relate to Him? Here, we can use Matthew 7, where Jesus is trying to get it into our hard heads that God *wants* to be bothered by our little needs and worries. He wants to be asked:

> Ask and it will be given to you; seek and you will find; knock and the door will be opened to you. For everyone who asks, receives; and the one who seeks, finds; and to the one who knocks, the door will be opened. Which one of you would hand his son a stone when he asks for a loaf of bread, or a snake when he asks for a fish? If you then, who are wicked, know how to give good gifts to your children, how much more will your heavenly Father give good things to those who ask him (Mt 7:7-11).

What kind of things should we ask our Father for? Well, Jesus told us what and how. We ask for what we most need. Every day. (Check out Matthew 6:9-13 for more!) What about fulfilling the Father's will? That is our way of loving Him. We have nothing that He needs, nothing we can give, so we praise Him and seek to do everything He asks of us.

> I suddenly remembered that no one can enter heaven except as a child; and nothing is so obvious in a child—not in a conceited child, but in a good child—as its great

> and undisguised pleasure in being praised . . . I am not forgetting . . . how very quickly, in my own experience, the lawful pleasure of praise from those whom it was my duty to please turns into the deadly poison of self-admiration. But I thought I could detect a moment—a very, very short moment—before this happened, during which the satisfaction of having pleased those whom I rightly loved and rightly feared was pure. And that is enough to raise our thoughts to what may happen when the redeemed soul, beyond all hope and nearly beyond belief, learns at last that she has pleased Him whom she was created to please.[3]

That C. S. Lewis quote makes me think of kids who keep "bothering" their dad ("Look, Dad, look!") as they jump into the pool or balance on a ledge. As sons, we thrive beneath the Father's loving gaze. Jesus Himself asked for nothing more. "You are my beloved Son; with you I am well pleased" (Mk 1:11).

> Jesus and Jesus alone is the Father's beloved. He has a unique relationship with His Father, which is his innermost meaning . . . The relationship of love that He has with His Father is to be shared with us. There is no other relationship we can claim. It is only by entering into Jesus's relationship with God that we can be in His heart. The only begotten is in the bosom of the Father, nearest to his heart; the beloved disciple is on the bosom of Jesus and drawn by him into the Father's heart, with him, where he is.[4]

Heart of a Father

As you learn to be a son, God will also be teaching you to be a father. During the past seven years (as I write this in my second-to-last year of theology), I have been asked to accompany some of the younger seminarians as a kind of academic coach for humanities studies and later on, for philosophy. At the moment, I also give spiritual direction to some of the altar servers at a local parish.

One habit I have formed over the past years is to always make a visit before the Eucharist prior to those moments when I will have to guide others. I ask Jesus for me to be His instrument, to say what He wants to be said through me. That way, I put myself on backstage and God, front and center.

We have only one Father: God. Yet we are called to participate in His fatherhood, full of Trinitarian self-giving. You must make the Father present to those children He has given you. Some of the most beautiful moments of my life have been when some of the younger seminarians approach and thank me for a book recommendation, for something I preached, or for an example of my own behavior—things that have helped them exactly how they needed at the time. Those moments make me feel very humble and grateful to God for having used me as a channel of His grace and love.

As a priest, you will exercise your fatherhood especially through the Mass, where you give your children their daily Bread, and in Confession, where the Father forgives His children and renews their strength. These are life-giving moments, moments of gift. God wants you to cherish and love your spiritual children—like Saint Paul. Just check out the intensity of some of these lines:

> My children, for whom I am again in labor until Christ be formed in you! (Gal 4:19)
>
> For God is my witness, how I long for all of you with the affection of Christ Jesus. (Phil 1:8)

> With such affection for you, we were determined to share with you not only the gospel of God, but our very selves as well, so dearly beloved had you become to us. . . . we treated each one of you as a father treats his children. (1 Thes 2:8, 11)

> I am writing you this not to shame you, but to admonish you as my beloved children. Even if you should have countless guides to Christ, yet you do not have many fathers, for I became your father in Christ Jesus through the gospel. Therefore, I urge you, be imitators of me. For this reason I am sending you Timothy, who is my beloved and faithful son in the Lord. (1 Cor 4:14-17)

Your fatherly love must always seek what is truly best for souls, and that is to bring them to God. A father gives everything and anything for his children, even that which he most loves. "He who did not spare his own Son but handed him over for us all, how will he not also give us everything else along with him?" (Rom 8:32)

A father guards and protects. In Exodus 17, Moses raises his hands in prayer to God. (When you are a priest, prayer is your primary strength.) His children, Israel, fight against the people of Amalek and win because Moses keeps his hands raised—with a bit of help from Aaron. Moses even stands between God and Israel when God wants to destroy the Israelites for making and worshiping the golden calf. "He would have decreed their destruction, had not Moses, his chosen one, Withstood him in the breach to turn back his destroying anger" (Ps 106:23).

Jesus also gives us the image of the Good Shepherd who goes after that one lost sheep to bring him back, who lays down His life for His sheep. A father waits for his child. His son might steal from him, abuse his trust, despise him, but a true father never gives up on his own. As in the parable of the prodigal son (Luke 15), the father waits for his son, day in and day out, and as soon as he sees his son on the road home, runs out to meet him. Had he pursued the prodigal and brought him home by force, there could have been no true reconciliation in freedom of heart.

A father gives dignity. Continuing with Luke's parable, "His son said to him, 'Father, I have sinned against heaven and against you; I no longer deserve to be called your son.' But his father ordered his servants, 'Quickly bring the finest robe and put it on him; put a ring on his finger and sandals on his feet'" (Lk 15:21-22). It does not matter that he has been betrayed or embarrassed before his neighbor; the father will never be ashamed of his son. And he shows it by giving him back his status within the household.

Lastly, Saint Joseph can teach us so much about fatherhood. He was not a physical father but a father by vocation to a son that belonged to someone else. Sound familiar? He accepted his mission, protected and defended Our Lord and Mary, worked to feed them. If Mary gave Jesus His body and Jesus shared our nature through her, Joseph raised Jesus to be a man. He taught Jesus virtues, work, and the Scriptures—perhaps not as well as a scribe but as well as he could. He guided Jesus's hands in the woodshop as together, they built tables and put the finishing touches on benches. He formed

Our Lord and at once, faded into the background. He holds a minimal place in the Gospels. You are called to be a faithful father, to form and shape Christ in souls and then slip into the background, unnoticed and often unthanked. Only eternity will reveal the depth of your sacrifice and love.

The highest vocation of a man is to be a father; and at least, in the most obvious sense, you have given that up. Yet, fatherhood means fruitfulness, life passing through you into this world. You are called to be fruitful. You are called to be a father. The task of pouring spiritual life into souls and calling them toward eternity surpasses anything you or I could ever manage. Luckily, none of this depends on us. We become representatives of the One Father in heaven. Those we deal with are His children, and He wants to give them life through us. What a relief! They are in His hands! So is our mission and calling.

Recommended Reading

Fathered by God: Learning What Your Dad Could Never Teach You by John Eldredge. God helps overcome any father wound and teaches us Himself how to become a man.

The Prodigal God: Recovering the Heart of the Christian Faith by Timothy Keller. This is my favorite book on Luke 15, showing how this parable contains, in a nutshell, the whole Gospel message.

Living in the Father's Embrace: Experiencing the Love at the Heart of the Trinity by George T. Montague, SM. This book is a simple invitation to trust.

NOTES

1. See John 15:16.
2. A Benedictine Monk, *In Sinu Iesu: When Heart Speaks to Heart, The Journal of a Priest at Prayer*, (Brooklyn, NY: Angelico Press, 2016), 12.
3. C. S. Lewis, *The Weight of Glory* (San Francisco: HarperOne, 2001), 36-37.
4. Ruth Burrows, OCD, *To Believe in Jesus*, (London: Sheed and Ward, 1978), 17-18.

CHAPTER 12
BREAD OF LIFE

The memory of the "boy with the bread," as Katniss calls Peeta throughout *The Hunger Games* trilogy, has seared itself into her memory as the time when she regained her hope in life. She was starving, and Peeta burned loaves of bread on purpose so she could collect what Peeta's mother could not sell. The bread means life for her family and a beating for Peeta. Katniss cannot understand why he would have done something for someone he did not know that well.[1] Throughout the tale, Peeta often appears associated with bread, and bread means life. Peeta makes sure Katniss gets that bread and takes a beating for it.

I think this story is a helpful image for what the Eucharist gives us. We receive it from heaven, having done nothing to merit it, and the gift invites us to enter deeper into a relationship with this God who has taken the form of bread and offered Himself as sacrifice to give us life. You are called to eat of this bread and give it out to God's children. It is the key to priestly holiness.

Why has God given us this bread? To sustain us on the journey, to give us heaven itself, the goal of our journey, though now we do not fully realize it. Elijah was told by the angel to eat else the way would be too long for him.

The Mass

"For I received from the Lord what I also handed on to you, that the Lord Jesus, on the night he was handed over, took bread" (1 Cor 11:23).

In the Liturgy of the Mass, we slip through time's cracks into eternity; God reaches into our "now" and pulls us into Himself. We are joined to God and the whole Church through prayer over two thousand years old.

As a priest, I will live my Mass either as a functionary or as a lover. The functionary goes through the motions because that is his job. He has perfected his routine and seeks to celebrate Mass in the most effective way, giving priority to speed, being entertaining, etc. For the functionary, time during Mass passes much too slowly, or it passes quickly because he is distracted with other things.

The priest-lover does not seek to be "effective" so much as to offer himself and all God's people with Christ in his offering to the Father. The lover does not merely follow the rubrics; he tries to live and breathe them, before the altar and in every moment of his life. He does not enter into routine during Mass but into relationship. Time is not his focus as he celebrates the mystery and offers up himself with Christ the Victim.

> Jesus has left with us a sacred rite whereby his perfect surrender to his Father, enacted all his life long, reaching its climax in his death, is concretised at a specific moment here for us; for us, precisely, so that we can deliberately, with most full intent make it our own. In the mass we

> have the deepest expression of what prayer is. Here God does everything. Here Jesus, his beloved, offers himself, the perfect offering of perfect love in which his Father delights. He delights in it because it gives him the supreme, eagerly desired opportunity to lavish himself on man. . . . If we want God, if we really long for union with him, then we shall want the mass with all the passion of our hearts.[2]

Only the Eucharist can satisfy your infinite longings, your hunger for God; God's children are hungry for the Bread of Life—He calls you to feed them. So, the Mass answers both your need for God and gives meaning to your zeal for souls.

Only the priest says "Father" *in persona Christi* until the doxology, the offering up of the sacrifice to the Father. After that offering up, heaven and earth are reunited and all of us are able to say, "Our Father." Heaven becomes present, though it remains invisible. If only we had eyes to see! Along with the Liturgy of the Hours, the Mass sustains the priest and fills his life with meaning and direction: his life becomes part of the Life given for the world.

Adoration

A while ago, another seminarian and I were preparing breakfast for the next day and speaking about prayer. One of his comments left me perplexed. I had mentioned the importance of spending time in the chapel. He told me, "I don't really feel the need to spend time before the Eucharist in adoration. When I want to pray, I go outside and walk around. Contact with nature helps me pray better."

Now, I would never deny the importance of finding God in nature—I really think it is essential! But to systematically prefer a walk outside to a quiet moment in the chapel seems a bit strange to me. I mean, you cannot understand the priesthood without the Eucharist, so I have always thought a good priest should be something of a Eucharistic addict. He may not always have the time for an extra hour with Our Lord, but his heart is there.

An image I heard many years ago has helped me value adoration time: the Eucharist is like the microwave for sanctity. Simply being in Jesus's presence transforms me little by little. One of my favorite prayers when I don't feel like praying is, "Lord, change me in spite of me!" And He has, at His own pace, but He has.

In my seminary, we have Jesus exposed in our chapel every afternoon until evening prayer. I do not always get around to it; but each afternoon, I try to get in an extra half hour with Jesus, especially if I have lots of things to do. It helps me realize that God is the center of my life and that time "wasted" with Him can never be fruitless. I think of some of my closest friendships over the years. Sure, I have talked lots with them, but maybe the best moments have simply been being together, sharing the same experiences. Likewise, those moments of silence with Our Lord will help you to learn to listen and truly find rest in the silence. Alone with Jesus, you give Him the opportunity for intimacy.

Then, there are moments of community adoration when we all gather together for a half hour at the day's end to pray Compline and receive Benediction. There are evenings (frequently) when I do not feel like being there, when I would rather be in bed or doing something "interesting"—those are my "change-me-in-spite-of-me" moments. But there are other evenings when I feel myself uplifted by and united with so many of the other seminarians in my community. The Eucharist unites us more powerfully than anything else in the universe. And, though some may not "feel" it, the presence of each one supports the others.

Sacrament of Love

The first time I went to the *Corpus Christi* procession in Bolsena, I wasn't expecting much. The year before I had been to Orvieto, with the famous Eucharistic miracle and a procession full of people dressed in medieval attire: knights, ladies-in-waiting, peasants, princes, trumpet fanfares, pomp, and pageantry. Bolsena, I had been told, was just flowers scattered along the path. Yet these two cities were at the heart and start of devotion to the Blessed Sacrament: the miracle happened in 1263 at Bolsena, where a host bled onto a corporal at Mass. The corporal was then moved to Orvieto. Within a year, Pope Urban IV proclaimed the Feast of Corpus Christi, and Saint Thomas Aquinas wrote its Liturgy, a masterwork of poetry and praise.

So, I found myself at Bolsena, and the procession started—no trumpets or costumes here. Yet, in between the two lines of the procession were mosaics made from flower petals showing different religious scenes, saints, and virtues. I marveled as we in the procession passed, impressed with the artwork. We seminarians were right ahead of the priests; and soon, I looked back toward the priest carrying the monstrance with Our Lord. What I saw amazed me. The two lines of the procession walked on either side around the flower mosaics—the priest with Jesus walked *on* them. All that loving preparation, all the beauty and artwork, culminating in the moment when Jesus would pass by, and the flowers would be destroyed.

What is the Eucharist? Do I have that kind of faith that gives everything to God for the sake of that moment when He passes by? God gives Himself for my food—can I not give Him everything He asks, make my life a sacrifice like His? The Eucharist teaches us to love with Christ's Heart. I received the ministry of acolyte a little over four months ago (as I first write these lines), and there came a week when I was assigned to help distribute communion at Mass to the other seminarians. Spontaneously, I started praying for each person on whose lips I placed the Host: "Lord, I don't love this person as You want me to love him." This simple prayer was both an act of contrition and a plea that He teach me to love, that He love through me (in spite of me).

> The Eucharist is the heart and center of the priest's intimacy with God, not only the center, but the intense furnace of his affective life and the laser-point of the meaning of his whole existence. The experience of the Eucharist is the living source of the indescribable joy that shakes his being to its very depths and keeps him continually conscious of the magnitude of God. In the celebration of the Eucharist, pondering the dimensions of this mystery, the inward eye is opened; and the moral gaze is sharpened and made fully aware. This mystic communion with God and our own openness to savor the full meaning of what we encounter digs a deep world of interiority. From this life of priestly interiority comes a persistent sharing in Christ's own spousal self-giving to the Church.[3]

Recommended Reading

Jesus and the Jewish Roots of the Eucharist: Unlocking the Secrets of the Last Supper by Brant Pitre. This study shows how much of our Liturgy comes from Jewish liturgy, helping us to better understand how the one was prepared by the other.

The Wellspring of Worship by Jean Corbon. This book gives a theological/existential presentation of the Liturgy that steeps the reader in mystery, longing, and reverence.

In Sinu Iesu: When Heart Speaks to Heart—The Journal of a Priest at Prayer by a Benedictine Monk. A priest and Our Lord both open their hearts to each other: an excellent help for adoration.

I guess instead of a lot of reading, the best thing I can do is recommend that you spend time in silence *with Him.*

Notes

1. Suzanne Collins, *The Hunger Games* (New York: Scholastic Inc., 2009), 31.
2. Ruth Burrows, *To Believe in Jesus* (London: Sheed and Ward, 1978), 80.
3. David L. Ricken, *Be Thou My Vision* (Omaha: IPF Publications, 2009), 125-126.

CHAPTER 13
SENSE OF THE NOW: FORMATION

Thirty years. Jesus spent thirty years in Nazareth and only three in public ministry. Do the math. Would it not have been better to have started working miracles and preaching right away as the apocryphal gospels would have us believe? We can guess that Jesus knew the purpose of His life and started preparing for it at least by the time He was twelve. That is when He runs away from His family to do some "pastoral work" in the temple. He knows what His life is about. But then, He goes back home and according to Luke, obeys them, growing in wisdom and stature before God and men. Some eighteen years later, He begins His public life.

Formation for the priesthood lasts years; and a lot of times, you might get frustrated: *I am wasting my time here! I have given my life to following Our Lord, and here I am stuck in the four walls of the seminary—classes, meals, work . . . What is the purpose of it all?* Maybe you do not think these thoughts explicitly; but speaking for myself, at least, there have been a lot of times when I have caught myself living out this kind of mindset in my day-to-day life. Routine leads us to frustration. It definitely does not help us toward the purpose of our formation: preparing ourselves for the mission and growing deeper in our relationship with Jesus. Routine leads to chronic superficiality: not seizing each moment to grow and to give our all to God.

So why did Jesus wait so long to start to save us? The answer is that He didn't. Saint Paul tells us that Jesus was obedient unto death—that is what won us our salvation, the sacrifice that the Father asks of us as well: obedience. God takes care of making it fruitful. So, Christ's whole life was dedicated to saving us—we will not "get it" unless we learn to see Christ's life and ours with eyes of faith. This implies an attitude of *being* over *doing*. I have given my life to God, so I am here to do whatever He wants. Seminary is a time to forge the priest I will be for the rest of my life. It is a time to develop that intimacy with God that will sustain me in all the good that I do and keep me from falling into burnout. Formation is about digging the foundations of my life; it allows me to keep building and growing through all my priesthood.

Cardinal Van Thuan had to learn this courage and faith the hard way. He was imprisoned by the Vietnamese communists for thirteen years, and in his book *Five Loaves and Two Fish*, he tells how he was at first very frustrated with his inability to reach his people.[1] Then, he received a light that he needed to choose God over God's works and if God's works were taken away by imprisonment or other circumstances, he could grow in love for God Himself. God must be the center of your life—then you can worry about God's works.

Putting the Pieces Together

Where to start? What is the basis of your formation or any person's formation? You guessed it—human formation. Check out numbers 63 and 94 of the 2016 *Ratio Fundamentalis* for information about priestly formation:

> For priestly formation, the importance of human formation cannot be sufficiently emphasized. Indeed, the holiness of a priest is built upon it and depends, in large part, upon the authenticity and maturity of his humanity. . . . This will make them a living reflection of the humanity of Jesus and a bridge that unites people with God.[2]

> Human formation, being the foundation of all priestly formation, promotes the integral growth of the person and allows the integration of all its dimensions.[3]

Now, each person, when we speak about formation, is like a plate; and human formation is like the plate's base. (No laughter, please—I thought up this image all by myself.) Growing in human formation is like increasing the diameter of the plate. When we are talking about human formation, I especially mean the formation of your will, conscience, and affectivity. A strong will gives you the ability to sacrifice yourself for God and others, to overcome temptation and grow in virtue, to make your obedience to God something worthwhile. A well-formed conscience enables you to live in sincerity before God, others, and yourself, to live according to who you are. Only in this way can you become a prophet and witness to Christ who is Truth itself.

Maybe you can see where this is headed. What is the purpose of the plate? To put food on it of course! Since I'm in Italy right now, we'll go with a nice plate of steamy *pasta alla carbonara* cooked *al dente*. And the bigger your plate is, the better: the more pasta you can put on it! What would the pasta be? Your spiritual formation—God himself. (Forgive me, Lord, for any possible irreverence.)

The purpose of your life is to grow closer to God and eventually, be with Him forever in eternity. The plate exists for the pasta, in order to help nourish you and others. "But what about apostolate?" you may protest. We will get there.

This plate image helps us see how each person is created completely for God, and forming yourself into the best person you can be naturally prepares you for a deep encounter with God and enables you to draw closer to Him.

Good news! You in your specific vocation are not called to be just a plate but (drumroll please) a bowl! As a priest, God is also asking you to form yourself intellectually.

A bowl with tall sides increases exponentially the dish's space for pasta—it really gives you a lot more capacity. In this way, your studies are meant to help bring you closer to God and, thus, contribute to your formation as a more complete human person. *"But what about apostolate?" you ask.* We will get there.

Now, there are some saints in the Church who have little or almost no intellectual formation; they are like plates with extremely wide diameters and fit more pasta than you or I will likely ever manage. There are others, however, who are very intelligent and capable in the intellectual field, whose sides are very high on the bowl. But if they lack the human formation aspect (virtue, the capacity for sacrifice, sincerity in their efforts, etc.), they are missing the plate bottom. The pasta falls through and almost nothing stays except maybe a bit of sauce or a noodle stuck to the bowl's sides. Saints without intellectual formation know God far better than the intellectual who is not a saint. But as priests, God calls us to have both spiritual and intellectual depth. One aspect, however, is more essential than the other.

Some of what you study will seem to have little or no use for the apostolate, but you need to consider that you are not studying *only* for the mission. You see, our studies help us grow in our knowledge of different truths. And the truth (as you will or have seen in philosophy) is analogous. It points toward the Truth itself, who is God. So, any small truth you learn here in the seminary is opening you up, preparing the soil for God's truth.

Since you are studying for a lot of your seminary life, how you live that aspect of your formation will have a huge impact on your human, spiritual, and pastoral life. For example, if you cannot concentrate for over five minutes in your study, chances are your prayer life suffers too when you try to meditate.

With regard to pastoral formation, explaining the faith requires a deep preparation and understanding of it. You can study just to pass your exams, or you can study because you need to prepare yourself to be the best instrument of God that you can be. In our bowl of pasta image, pastoral formation is the fork—that which "transmits" the pasta to the mouths hungry for God. In order to be able to give God to others in pastoral work, we must first be filled with God. Saint Thomas Aquinas says in the *Summa* that apostolate is the sharing of what we have contemplated.[4] Saint Paul himself shares his conversion story four times in the New Testament, and Saint John the Evangelist tells us, "What was from the beginning, what we have heard, what we have seen with our eyes, what we looked upon and touched with our hands concerns the Word of life what we have seen and heard we proclaim now to you" (1 Jn 1:1). A priest seeks to fill himself with God so he can give God to others.

The priest is the bowl. His entire vocation and existence are for the sake of those God wishes to nourish through his priests, for the sake of the whole world! The priest's whole being shouts aloud his mission! This is what formation is all about.

No one will be perfect after ordination, but you should have reached the place in your journey that God wants for you at that moment. Getting there might be difficult because of the circumstances and difficulties God allows in your life, but ultimately, your role is essential. And you are living it *now*. You have to want it and, with the grace of God, work toward it. "So whoever is in Christ is a new creation: the old things have passed away; behold, new things have come" (2 Cor 5:17).

Recommended Reading

A little bit of everything here . . .

Five Loaves and Two Fish by Francis Xavier Nguyan Van Thuan. Written from prison. My favorite part is his reflection on the difference between God and God's work.

Pastores Dabo Vobis by Saint John Paul II. This document gives us the basics of priestly formation today.

The Gift of the Priestly Vocation by the Congregation for the Clergy: obviously.

The Little Prince by Antoine de Saint-Exupéry. This is a classic tale of relationships, priorities, simplicity.

Why Priests Are Happy: A Study of the Psychological and Spiritual Health of Priests by Stephen J. Rossetti. What kind of habits and worldviews make for happy priests?

NOTES

1. Francis Xavier Nguyen Van Thuan, *Five Loaves and Two Fish: Meditations on the Eucharist* (St. Louis, MO: Pauline Books and Media, 2003).
2. Congregation for the Clergy, *The Gift of the Priestly Vocation*, Vatican City 2016, sec.63, http://www.clerus.va/content/dam/clerus/Ratio%20Fundamentalis/The%20Gift%20of%20the%20Priestly%20Vocation.pdf (accessed 1 December 2017).
3. Ibid., sec. 94.
4. Thomas Aquinas, Summa (see III, q.40, a.1, ad2)

Chapter 14
A Lover of Beauty

Beauty and God

I am sitting in my room, looking west over a small valley that separates me from the next wave of Roman hills and, beyond them, the sunset. Day slips away as I try to put on paper a topic that has escaped me for the last several weeks of writer's block: beauty. I want to tell you that you need it, that you must long for it and seek it. Journeying into beauty means a greater understanding of your heart and of what you were made for.

We all agree that heaven is the goal of our lives: the contemplation of God. What is contemplation if not gazing on beauty, desiring beauty, and in a mysterious way, somehow being united with beauty? God is Beauty itself. The book of Psalms tells us that "the heavens declare the glory of God; the firmament proclaims the works of his hands" (Ps 19:2). Saint Augustine wrote of his search:

> And what is this God? I asked the earth, and it answered, "I am not he"; and everything in the earth made the same confession. I asked the sea and the deeps and the creeping things, and they replied, "We are not your God;

> seek above us." I asked the fleeting winds, and the whole air with its inhabitants answered, " . . . I am not God." I asked the heavens, the sun, moon, and stars; and they answered, "Neither are we the God whom you seek." And I replied to all these things which stand around the door of my flesh: "You have told me about my God, that you are not he. Tell me something about him." And with a loud voice they all cried out, "He made us."[1]

Hints of who an artist is can always be found in his handiwork—the Great Artist's trademark is beauty: "For from the greatness and the beauty of created things their original author, by analogy, is seen" (Ws 13:5).

While I look out over this sunset, my intellect understands something of what I am seeing, yet the experience is always beyond what my mind can grasp. This beauty awakens in my heart the desire to keep gazing, to possess the moment forever; but it is beyond my strength to possess a sunset . . . always beyond, pointing to the Infinitely Beyond, God Himself.

Saint John Chrysostom once wrote that the beauty of creation can become a ladder through which we can reach God. A man who learns to contemplate beauty opens himself to finding God's echo in creatures, and finding God in all things teaches him to love them properly.

Sometimes we can be distracted by the fireworks in our lives: big, colorful, and loud. They are a way to celebrate extraordinary occasions such as the New Year or Independence Day. Some people live for fireworks, chasing after special moments that stand out but pass by quickly. Now, I have nothing against fireworks. Sometimes, we need to shout out our joy and clap at those bright shapes in the sky.

But a step beyond "firework" people would be "sunset" people: those who have learned to contemplate beauty. A sunset happens in silence, slowly, while most are so caught up in what they are doing that they continue on, unaware of the miracle taking place in the sky. A sunset surprises no one—it happens all the time and, so, is not worth much attention. See the difference? Cultivating an appreciation for beauty in your life helps to see even the little "normal" things for what they really are: secret bearers of beauty. Elijah did not find God in the earthquake, the fire, or the hurricane winds but in a soft breeze.

Once we get into the habit of allowing beauty to bring us to God, we start finding it everywhere! We start falling more and more in love with the Beauty behind all beauty; our hearts become centered on God. "O God, you are my God—it is you I seek! For you my body yearns; for you my soul thirsts" (Ps 63:2). Beauty trains our hearts for heaven.

Muriel Barbery wrote a novel called *The Elegance of the Hedgehog*, centered on a friendship between a cleaning woman named Renée and Paloma, the daughter of a very wealthy family. Paloma concludes the story with her own definition of beauty. In spite of sorrow, moments of beauty spring up and suspend time, the *always* within the *never*.[2] Maybe we could change her conclusion to say that beauty is the *always* within the *not yet*.

Beauty and Others

Most photographers love the "golden hour" when we do not see as we normally see during the day; but with the rising or setting sun at our backs, we somehow seize the light for our own. We are granted a glimpse at the magic in creation: each tree becomes a song and each leaf, a note. All is transformed, and even the most insipid and everyday sights become worthy in our eyes. The golden hour gives a quick glimpse at the truth of creation, at the beauty flowing through it all. God allows us somehow to see things bathed in His love that sustains and recreates.

We can say that we have grown in our perception of beauty when we have learned to see things as God sees them, with the setting sun at our backs. This applies especially to people! When God sees a person, He sees a goodness, a beauty beyond anything we could ever imagine. This goes way beyond the physical—just look at a photo of Mother Teresa smiling and tell me she is not beautiful! Yet only the pure in heart can see it. Those too centered on sensual beauty—an idolatry of the body—cannot perceive the deeper moral beauty. Only the pure in heart can start to see as God sees; only the pure in heart can see God:

> The summit, the archetype of beauty manifests itself in the face of the Son of Man crucified on the Cross of sorrows, Revelation of infinite love of God who, in His mercy for His creatures, restores beauty lost with original sin.[3]

To help us dig deeper into the importance of discovering and contemplating beauty in people, I am going to be relying on what Hans Urs von Balthasar presents in his book *Theo-Logic: The Truth of the World* about human knowledge and relationships. There are two ways of looking at someone: with justice or with mercy. A look of justice is a human and rational way of considering someone. On the one hand, we see (a part of) the person's reality: Paul is a drunk. He staggers home each night expecting his wife to take care of him after having squandered whatever he has earned . . . you get the idea. On the other hand, we see the person's ideal: Paul had it all going for him—he had a Harvard scholarship, supportive parents and friends, a loving wife. He should be a respectable man and a devoted father and husband. Justice sees the reality and the ideal and notes the difference between the two. Sure, no one is perfect, but some people are *really* not perfect. This look of justice gives us a certain truth, but it is far from the whole truth.

The look of mercy does not pretend the objective reality does not exist, but instead of seeing the distance between the two, mercy looks at reality *through* the ideal. What does this mean? When God created Paul, He created him with an incredible love and planned great things for him, the most important being that he become a saint. Paul's ideal is simply what God planned and wanted for him—seen in and through Christ. Mercy does not condemn because of the difference but is able to see with God the beauty hidden in this person, the potential there for holiness and conversion. Only a lover can know someone truly—God knows, loves, and sees something so beautiful in each person that He thought them worth creating and was willing to die for them. "But God proves his love for us in that while we were still sinners Christ died for us" (Rm 5:8).

When I know that I am loved, I try to live better, to become worthy of that love. I am valued, so I believe in my value. Or as Father Thomas Dubay writes, "Agape love is a gratuitous concern for the other for his own sake. It does not simply respond to goodness already present. It creates goodness where goodness was absent."[4] Love does not follow worthiness—it creates it.

As a priest, I must learn to see souls as God sees them, to glimpse the beauty and glory hidden behind their rags and their sin. Only then can I love them, accompany them, and help them grow in grace and beauty.

Recommended Reading

The Evidential Power of Beauty: Science and Theology Meet by Thomas Dubay, SM. This introduction to the theme of beauty investigates it from a philosophical and scientific perspective.

Theo-Logic: The Truth of the World by Hans Urs von Balthasar. This study can be hard to get through but is definitely worth it—especially the parts on how we understand and get to know others.

"The Feeling of Things, the Contemplation of Beauty" by Joseph Cardinal Ratzinger (24-30 August, 2002). Cardinal Ratzinger asks what is beauty and how it will save the world: (http://www.vatican.va/roman_curia/congregations/cfaith/documents/rc_con_cfaith_doc_20020824_ratzinger-cl-rimini_en.html).

"The *Via Pulchritudinis*, Way of Beauty" by the Pontifical Council for Culture (2009). This document explains how the best way to evangelize culture is through beauty, (http://www.cultura.va/content/cultura/en/pub/documenti/ViaPulchritudinis.html).

And an article of my own on beauty:

"The Status of Transcendental Beauty according to Saint Thomas Aquinas," my dissertation paper for licentiate in philosophy (https://www.academia.edu/13080724/The_Status_of_Transcendental_Beauty_according_to_Saint_Thomas_Aquinas).

NOTES

1. Augustine, *Confessions*, book X, https://www.ling.upenn.edu/courses/hum100/augustinconf.pdf, [22/1/17].

2. Muriel Barbery, *The Elegance of the Hedgehog* (New York: Europa Editions, 2008).

3. "The *Via Pulchritudinis*, Way of Beauty," http://www.cultura.va/content/cultura/en/pub/documenti/ViaPulchritudinis.html, (accessed 23 January 2018).

4. Thomas Dubay, *Authenticity: A Biblical Theology of Discernment* (San Francisco: Ignatius Press, 1997), 150.

Chapter 15
Communicating Christ

"Then he said to me, Son of man, go now to the house of Israel, and speak my words to them" (Ez 3:4). The priest preaches Christ as one sent: in the name of the Church and for the sake of the Church. It is not just me and Jesus against the world.

I used to have a hard time with the concept of love for the Church. It did not invoke much enthusiasm from me as it made me think of the hierarchy, the church buildings . . . some great anonymous mass of structures that one had to be a part of in order to follow Jesus. So I accepted the theory, but my attitude was that of someone paying rent in order not to be thrown out of his rooms. Sure, I had the duty to love and work for the Church, and I tried to fulfill that duty, even if half-heartedly.

But once I started thinking of the Church in terms of the concrete people around me, love for the Church took on whole new meaning. It became meaningful and urgent and translated into a desire to give Christ to everyone: "If I preach the gospel, this is no reason for me to boast, for an obligation has been imposed on me, and woe to me if I do not preach it!" (1 Cor 9:16). Sort of like the typical action film: the hero is needed, begged for help but stays indifferent until someone harms or threatens those he loves. Then the hero commits himself fully and personally to the cause (think Braveheart).

We have already touched on some of the sacraments previously. And, of course, we need to bring our souls to prayer and there, help them to carry their burdens and win graces for them. Here, I would like to share some thoughts on pastoral work as a communication of Christ: our preaching through example and, of course, through word.

Pope Francis tells us in numbers 265 and 266 of *Evangelii Gaudium*:

> We have a treasure of life and love which cannot deceive, and a message which cannot mislead or disappoint. It penetrates to the depths of our hearts, sustaining and ennobling us. It is a truth which is never out of date because it reaches that part of us which nothing else can reach. . . . It is impossible to persevere in a fervent evangelization unless we are convinced from personal experience that it is not the same thing to have known Jesus as not to have known him, not the same thing to walk with him as to walk blindly, not the same thing to hear his word as not to know it, and not the same thing to contemplate him, to worship him, to find our peace in him, as not to.[1]

Preaching with Your Life

If you remember the image of the "formation bowl," our pastoral work is the "fork" we use to help others eat the "pasta": the communication to souls of what we have contemplated and assimilated of God. Of course, the fruits depend on God, but we need to have the best bowl and fork available for God to work with. I'm putting these thoughts on example here because of the famous story of Saint Francis and Brother Leo who went to "preach" walking through the town without saying anything, the moral being to preach always and, if necessary, use words.

Pastoral "success" is impossible for us to measure on the supernatural plane. Perhaps that priest who has tried dozens of different initiatives, each one failing spectacularly, has had more spiritual success (i.e., has been used by grace to bring souls to God) than the priest with the touch of Midas. People tend not to want to work with the first one and flock to the second, yet . . .

In the novel *The Horse and His Boy*, C. S. Lewis tells the story of Shasta, an orphan who is trying to escape Calormen, the country where he is enslaved, and reach Narnia. On his journey, he and his friends discover that Calormen has sent a speedy force to take Narnia's southern ally, Archenland, by surprise. So, Shasta must bear this urgent message to Archenland and try to warn King Lune before it is too late. Fortunately, King Lune believes Shasta's message—why? Because Shasta has put his life on the line to get it to the king, something nearly impossible to fake. And the message is one of life or death.[2]

Your people can tell if you are authentic, if you believe in your message and back it up with your life, if you really love those entrusted to you or if you are a "mercenary shepherd" out to promote yourself and your agenda. You might, at times, fool yourself and perhaps even a few others, yet God sees the heart and God gives the fruit.

Benedict XVI reminds us:

> For the priest, then, being the "voice" of the Word is not merely a functional aspect. On the contrary, it implies a substantial "losing of himself" in Christ, participating with his whole being in the mystery of Christ's death and Resurrection: his understanding, his freedom, his will and the offering of his body as a living sacrifice (cf. Rm 12: 1-2). Only participation in Christ's sacrifice, in his kenosis, makes preaching authentic! And this is the way he must take with Christ to reach the point of being able to say to the Father, together with Christ: let "not what I will, but what you will" be done (Mk 14: 36). Proclamation, therefore, always involves self-sacrifice, a prerequisite for its authenticity and efficacy.[3]

Preparing to Preach

When the priesthood first entered my head at the ripe old age of five or six, I remember fascination with the idea of celebrating Mass. Though I had no clear idea of what the Eucharist really was, the mystery of it all somehow had captured my heart. However, one thing I absolutely did not want to do, ever, was to preach. I planned on becoming a priest and celebrating the Mass, all well and good. Yet I would surely be able to get someone else to take care of that preaching thing called the homily, right?

Well, God has His sense of humor because during my apostolic internship, I was assigned to be a professor of humanistic studies at our seminary in Connecticut; and there, I had to teach homiletics. But I had realized that God had given me some talent in the area of communication. By my last year of teaching, I had reorganized the seminary's entire two-year program for writing and public speaking. So I have a lot of suggestions (and pet peeves) to share with you. Of course, there will be other opinions out there on much of this stuff, so do not take everything in this chapter as written in stone.

1. Your preaching preparation should revolve around listening to God's Word—yes, a type of discernment! You discover what the Holy Spirit wants to say to His people through you. You are not the protagonist, either during your preparation or your delivery.

On the one hand, there are times when you need to give the congregation a specific message or lesson regarding their concrete circumstances, but just as often (if not more), we need to approach homily preparation without any previous planning.

Most of us tend to lean toward communicating our own ideas. For example, the Gospel of Peter walking on the water has to do with faith in Christ, so I use the Gospel as a springboard to talk about faith and what it means to me. Or I want to talk about faith, determining the topic before I have even read the readings and then figuring out a way to tie the readings in.

We need to learn to become listeners of the Word. If you are always "choosing" your themes without first listening to God, perhaps you will miss new richness in the text God wants to give you as He nourishes His people.

So, the first step to preparing a homily or any sort of religious talk should be prayer—take the Gospel to the chapel and pray with Our Lord about it; brainstorm about thc passage together with the desire to communicate whatever it is that He wishes: "I do nothing on my own, but I say only what the Father taught me" (Jn 8:28).

2. Another element to your preaching preparation will be study—you will never know all there is to know about Scripture, so keep going deeper. This enriches both your personal prayer life and your preaching. During my theology, I have had to do several papers on the Synoptic Gospels, the prophets and Saint Paul (so far). Each paper I have done has been enriching because I have deepened my knowledge of a specific passage and discovered treasures I had never suspected. In no way do I ever feel I have exhausted a passage; and if I have gotten so much out of so few verses, how much more awaits in the rest of the Bible!

3. You need to develop your personal style. It is usually helpful to start out imitating some of your favorite preachers and then, little by little, develop your own way of preaching that is really you. Learn to use your specific personality and its strengths. The person at the pulpit should not be different from the person in an everyday conversation.

4. If you can, practice your homilies or talks out loud beforehand—your ear will catch errors your eye misses; and usually, you will make key changes after going through it one or two times.

5. The last step before actually preaching is placing it all in Mary's hands. She gave Jesus to the world and will help us give Jesus through our words.

Preaching the Word

Every time I have to speak in public, I get nervous, no matter how well I have prepared. But that is okay, since it is God who has to be the protagonist. I have listened to him and try to say just what he wishes and nothing more. Here are a few random thoughts on the moment of preaching itself.

You need to be convinced of your message and its urgency: "My people need to hear this—it is life or death!" That attitude easily comes across in your preaching. As Saint Paul says, "The love of Christ impels us!" (2 Cor 5:14).

Share personal stories—they help you to be yourself and establish a more intimate connection with those listening.

One of the most helpful tools in preaching is your use of analogies (an image on steroids). You know, like in math: one is to two as fifty is to one hundred. The key concept is using one relationship between things we know to explain another relationship harder for us to understand. For example, you want to talk about the effect of grace in the soul. You could prepare your whole talk on the relationship between water and a field. The field needs water so it can give its harvest; the water falls from heaven freely without the field doing anything. Sure, no analogy is perfect, but the best ones help us go a little deeper into our faith.

Last of all, keep it short. Do us all a favor. Usually, it takes much more work to prepare a five-minute homily than a forty-minute one: each word has to count and fit perfectly with the others in order to convey the message . . . and fewer people will fall asleep.

In the end, whether we plant or water, God gives the fruit.

In *The Horse and His Boy*, Shasta delivers his message to King Lune and gets separated from the king's company in the mountain fog. He then starts feeling sorry for himself because he has suffered so much in his journey, and everything has been too hard. He finds himself with a companion walking alongside him unseen in the mist and shares his troubles.[4]

He tells of all the dangers he and his friends have faced, especially the problem of the lions . . . and finds out his companion is a lion, the only lion Shasta has ever encountered on his journey. He is the lion who brought Shasta and his friends together for their quest; the lion who protected Shasta as he slept; the lion who inspired fear in the horses so they would go faster and reach King Lune on time; the lion who saved Shasta as a baby and brought him to his adopted home:

> "Who are you?" asked Shasta.
> "Myself," said the Voice, very deep and low so that the earth shook: and again "Myself," loud and clear and gay: and then the third time "Myself," whispered so softly you could hardly hear it, and yet it seemed to come from all round you as if the leaves rustled with it.[5]

In delivering his message, Shasta encounters the Message for whose sake he has suffered so much. He receives the answers to his deepest questions and longings and then can ask the most important question of all: "Who are you?"

The fruit is God's. The work is God's. We are instruments. Our preaching and lives should bring others to an encounter with the Word, before whom all we can do is adore and fall silent.

Recommended Reading

King's Cross: The Story of the World in the Life of Jesus by Timothy Keller. This book goes through the Gospel according to Mark in order to better understand the person of Jesus.

An Ignatian Introduction to Prayer: Scriptural Reflections According to the Spiritual Exercises by Timothy M. Gallagher, OMV. This book is especially for beginners but can also serve to teach others to meditate with the Gospels.

Evangelii Gaudium by Pope Francis. He speaks about how we need to bear witness to Christ through our lives; numbers 135-159 have some excellent homily suggestions.

NOTES

1. Francis, *Evangelii Gaudium* (2013), sec. 265, 266, http://w2.vatican.va/content/francesco/en/apost_exhortations/documents/papa-francesco_esortazione-ap_20131124_evangelii-gaudium.html#I.%E2%80%82The_entire_people_of_God_proclaims_the_Gospel.
2. C. S. Lewis, *The Horse and His Boy* (New York: Collier Books, 1978).
3. Benedict XVI, General Audience of 24 June 2009, http://w2.vatican.va/content/benedict-xvi/en/audiences/2009/documents/hf_ben-xvi_aud_20090624.html.
4. Lewis.
5. Ibid., 157-159.

CHAPTER 16
THE HOLY SPIRIT: MASTER ARTIST OF YOUR SOUL

"Behold, I stand at the door and knock. If anyone hears my voice and opens the door, [then] I will enter his house and dine with him, and he with me" (Rev 3:20). If we hear Him. If we open.

In *The Great Divorce*, C. S. Lewis takes us on a journey from hell to heaven in order to illustrate the all-or-nothing choice each person must make. Souls from "grey town" are taken by bus for a field trip to heaven, which they find contains more reality than they can initially handle. They are like ghosts in the real world, almost without substance. Heaven is reality, its grass too real for the visitors to bend beneath their feet, its flowers too strong to pluck. Heaven is too much for them . . . unless they be transformed.[1]

We can use this imagery to talk about growth in holiness, about the utter difference in experience between someone completely surrendered to the Holy Spirit and His work in the person's life and someone who clings . . . to little things. The difference is absolute. We will wither unless we grow under the Holy Spirit's guidance, unless we enter into that new reality, that undiscovered continent waiting to be explored.

At the Start

When we start off on our journey into holiness, much of the work depends on our own effort: overcoming sin, fighting to pay attention in prayer, sacrificing ourselves, etc. At this level, reason is master and guide. (Remember, human formation is the base of the bowl that is you.) It is easy to understand why we should overcome the sin that enslaves us and makes us bow to our lower desires. It makes perfect sense to form a strong will and to live in truth and coherence.

Sacrifice and obedience play a central role. God often needs to break the pot in order to remake it. We have our sins and tendencies toward evil that have to be purified, bad habits that must be overcome in order to follow Jesus. We learn to set aside our own plans (is there anything harder?) in order to obey. We fight to pray and can become content with a constant dryness in prayer—not really expecting or wanting anything more in our relationship with God.

We have to work at it; we have to fight for it. Yet behind the scenes, there is much more going on than we realize: "no one can say, 'Jesus is Lord,' except by the holy Spirit" (1 Cor 12:3). He is there, working in and through me though often I do not notice it.

Luckily, we can receive necessary help through spiritual direction, which God uses to keep us humble and trusting. Our spiritual directors help us recognize God's hand in our lives and take the needed steps toward God. And God invites us to keep growing. Whereas before, we had taken the initiative in our spiritual lives, there comes a point when God asks us to start letting go and letting Him take control. Very difficult.

Our reason has had to play a large role in avoiding vice and developing virtue; but eventually, reason simply is not enough. I know people who are the most reasonable people you could meet, extremely logical and sincerely open to listening to you and understanding. Yet they can fail to understand spiritual things, conclusions that cannot ever be reached by reason alone. Reason without faith can lead to perpetual mental circles without ever realizing that the complete truth may lie beyond reason's capacity to discern.

Breakthrough

In *The Great Divorce*, all the people who come from hell (which fits entirely into an imperceptible crack between a blade of grass or two in heaven) step into a reality that is much larger than anything they ever could have imagined. Naturally, fear possesses many of them. Others have to give up a prejudice or vice in order to be able to stay and thrive in heaven.

Lewis tells of one man-ghost with a red lizard on his shoulder, whispering in his ear and keeping the man enslaved to his passions. An angel offers to silence the lizard, and the ghost says it would like that but resists when he realizes the angel means to kill it. The ghost tries to put it off, saying that perhaps later they could consider it, that perhaps the lizard is not such a big deal after all. The angel insists, and the ghost says the angel would kill him if the lizard were to be killed. The angel cannot kill the lizard against the ghost's will. Finally, the ghost consents, screaming as the angel blasts the lizard. The ghost is transformed into a complete and real man, his lizard, into a magnificent stallion—so much more than he had hoped for. Full of joy, he leaps on the horse's back and gallops off into true life.[2]

This is just how it happens when God asks us to grow in abandonment to His will. "There is always something they insist on keeping even at the price of misery. There is always something they prefer to joy—that is, to reality."[3] The price of misery or of mediocrity: we cling to little things, often good things, instead of clinging to Him. He will not rip away what we hold on to, yet with our hands full, He cannot place Himself in them.

For most of my spiritual life, I had never prayed much to the Holy Spirit. Sure, we used to begin all our classes and activities with the "Come, Holy Spirit" prayer, but it never really meant much to me. The Holy Spirit was God (obviously), yet I never considered the possibility of a personal relationship with Him.

For several years now, I have known myself pretty well as far as my qualities and defects go. But as ordination gets closer and closer, the defects have become much more real and present for me. I have realized existentially (and not just theoretically) that as a priest, I will have to depend on God for everything because by myself, it is simply impossible.

The solution comes especially through the gifts of the Holy Spirit, who little by little reveals to you what kind of priest He wants you to be. He starts taking over, guiding, acting . . . especially in the little things! How beautiful to realize that He has been and is acting in your life when you look back at something you did and say, "Hey, that's not me. By myself, I never could have said that kind word when I was feeling angry or been open to changing what I had so carefully planned."

"Now the Lord is the Spirit, and where the Spirit of the Lord is, there is freedom. All of us, gazing with unveiled face on the glory of the Lord, are being transformed into the same image from glory to glory, as from the Lord who is the Spirit" (2 Cor 3:17-18). The Holy Spirit forms us into Christ! You can reach spiritual maturity only when you have learned to let Him guide your life. "When you were younger, you used to dress yourself and go where you wanted; but when you grow old, you will stretch out your hands, and someone else will dress you and lead you where you do not want to go" (Jn 21:18).

Living this way is exhilarating because you have really lost control. You can go only so far by your own effort, at a snail's pace. Like a roller coaster climbing slowly up the tracks, there comes a point where the deliberate work slips into second place and gravity takes over. Then, you just lift your hands and scream as you rush down and upside down: the exhilaratingly breathtaking sheer wonder of it all and the terror of the rushing wind.

That's sort of what happens when God takes over: a new form of trust where you have no idea what is going to happen, but you know you are in His hands. "Perfect love drives out fear" (1 Jn 4:18). After years of hints and promises, this is what you were created for: adventure, beauty, freedom in God, life in Christ! Imagine a roller coaster that tops the hill only to keep moving at the speed of the gears that keep it from going down too fast. It might be safe, secure, and constant, but the entire ride becomes pointless.

How does the Holy Spirit want to live, work, and pray through you? The gifts are His life within you, true life. One of the most consoling things I have learned about the gifts (in the book *I Want to See God*)[4] is that God will often give the gifts especially where there is a human lack.

Take me, for example. I tend to be very indecisive and constantly rethink practical decisions. Yet, at times, I sense that God has given me a bit of the gift of counsel, of seeing clearly what has to be done in my own life and also in the lives of others. Since I am weak in that area, it underlines all the more that it is God's work and not my own. (Keeps me humble!)

Then, there are the fruits of the Holy Spirit, which are what we are called to enjoy and long for, the good life! "The fruits of the Spirit are perfections that the Holy Spirit forms in us as the first fruits of eternal glory. The tradition of the Church lists twelve of them: 'charity, joy, peace, patience, kindness, goodness, generosity, gentleness, faithfulness, modesty, self-control, chastity.'"[5] Yet they are also signs that help us discern if what we are doing or living comes from God.

The Holy Spirit has a specific plan for you: for your sanctity and your priesthood. No one else could ever be the priest you are called to be or reflect that unique aspect of Christ that your sanctity is meant to make shine forth. So, another theme for prayer, especially as you draw closer to ordination, is to ask the Holy Spirit what kind of priest He wants you to be. He wants you to be a saint, to reflect in a unique way a part of the infinite beauty of Jesus. How does He want you to reflect Christ? What Beatitude, in particular, are you called to live? What Gospel scene or passage especially captures how He wants to form Christ in you?

At least, that is some of what I'm praying through right now: what kind of reflection of Christ does the Holy Spirit want to shape in me? So I hope and ask the Holy Spirit that these thoughts I have shared through this book help you on your journey. Please pray for me, that I be faithful to his call.

Pentecost Prayer

What do you want from me? What can I give you to make you happy? It's not the first time I have asked the question, Lord, and I will have to continue asking in order to go deeper into my answer. But there are times when what you ask of me is decisive. So, I ask again: What can I do? What do I lack? I want to overcome my mediocrity and half-hearted surrender. Show me the way.

And I know that so often, you hold back the answer, waiting to reply because I am not yet strong enough to say *yes*. Give me that strength, that grace to follow wherever You lead me. Then give me the answer as to what I must do. What must I do to become who You want me to be, to cast off my chains and fly with you beyond the sun?

But only say the word, and, in the moment of your grace, whisper the answer. And I will say yes with all my heart.

Take my life and make it yours for real. Blow away my vanity like morning mist and take the chains of my need to control everything and crush them! Because in controlling the conditions of my surrender, I am putting the limits of my small mind and heart on your plans for my life—always so much bigger than I could ever plan for. To break free means to let you take full control, to heal me and to be led by Your Holy Spirit living and moving in me.

Give what You ask, and ask whatever You will. I have no wings—you will have to lift me. My treasure in heaven is not enough to pay for the journey—you will have to pay my passage. I am blind, so You will have to lead me; a cripple, and so You must carry me in Your arms.

Come, Holy Spirit, and fill my heart! Give me a new Pentecost so with the Apostles, I can cast off fear and break out of that upper room to which I have limited myself—You call me to fill the world, whole nations, with Your love. And since we already plan to kill my little attachments, why not go all the way and shape me into another Christ: help me to know Him as only those who bear the Cross with Him know Him; help me to love Him with a heart pure as Mary's and filled with You who are Love itself; and help me follow in His path—to seek always the Father's glory—the path to total intimacy with and imitation of Him. Amen.

Recommended Reading

The Sanctifier by Luis M. Martínez. This inspiring and deep book on the Holy Spirit helps you understand His dreams for you and how He works in your life.

I Want to See God and *I Am a Daughter of the Church* by P. Marie-Eugène of the Child Jesus, OCD. This two-volume set synthesizes the doctrine of spiritual life of Saint Teresa of Ávila and Saint John of the Cross. It has taken me years to slowly understand, savor, and go through these books bit by bit.

The Great Divorce by C. S. Lewis. God or nothing. There is no in-between.

Discovering Your Personal Vocation: The Search for Meaning through the Spiritual Exercises by Herbert Alphonso, SJ. This short volume gives criteria to discern your personal vocation: how you are meant to uniquely imitate Christ.

NOTES

1. C. S. Lewis, *The Great Divorce* (London: Harper Collins, 2002), 20-21.
2. Ibid., 106-111.
3. Ibid., 71.
4. See P. Marie Eugène, OCD, *I Want to See God: A Practical Synthesis of Carmelite Spirituality* (Thomas More Publishing, 1998).
5. *The Catechism of the Catholic Church*, 1832, http://www.vatican.va/archive/ccc_css/archive/catechism/p3s1c1a7.htm (accessed 7 September 2017).

ACKNOWLEDGEMENTS

A big thanks to everyone who helped inspire this book: my family, Father Leo McCarthy, Father Álvaro Corcuera, Father Christopher Brackett, Father Justin Kielhorn, and many more priests. I started listing a lot of companions here, then realized that if I name any of you, I have to name more people than I can reasonably put here . . . and I prefer not to risk leaving one of you out. Anyways, you know who you are. Thank you with all my heart.

Thanks as well to those who helped review and critique this book—for your enthusiasm, patience, insights . . . and brotherhood! Dain Scherber, Luis Eduardo Rodríguez, Emmanuel Ortiz, Russell Ward, Gustavo Balestrin, Baltazar López, João Paulo García, and Nicholas Torrey.

Lastly, my gratitude to IPF for helping to get this book into the hands of seminarians; a particular thanks to Deacon James Keating, for his encouragement and Michelle Funke, for her editorial expertise and patience with this author!

www.ingramcontent.com/pod-product-compliance
Lightning Source LLC
LaVergne TN
LVHW040220110826
845146LV00005B/1358

* 9 7 9 8 8 8 8 7 0 4 1 9 6 *